PROTECTING
the
PRESIDENT

DAN BONGINO

PROTECTING

the

PRESIDENT

AN INSIDE ACCOUNT *of the* TROUBLED SECRET SERVICE
IN AN ERA *of* EVOLVING THREATS

 WND BOOKS

PROTECTING THE PRESIDENT

Published by WND Books, Washington, DC. WND Books is a registered trademark of WorldNetDaily.com, Inc. ("WND").

Book designed by Mark Karis

WND Books are available at special discounts for bulk purchases. WND Books also publishes books in electronic formats. For more information call (541) 474-1776, e-mail orders@wndbooks.com, or visit www.wndbooks.com.

Hardcover ISBN: 978-1-944229-86-3
eBook ISBN: 978-1-944229-87-0

Library of Congress Cataloging-in-Publication Data available upon request

Printed in the United States of America
17 18 19 20 21 22 LBM 9 8 7 6 5 4 3 2 1

Dedicated to the men and women of law enforcement. The brave guardians who selflessly put their lives on the line, defending us against the wolf pack.

CONTENTS

FOREWORD

If you ask any person living in America today what the United States Secret Service does, they will likely tell you, "They're the guys who protect the president," and that is true. Quite simply, the brave men and women of the Secret Service have an awesome responsibility: They are tasked with keeping the single most important person on Earth, The president of the United States, alive and well. The agency does all this while being an indirect representation to the office of the president, the White House and the people who are affiliated with the executive branch of our government (whether the Service wants to be that representation or not). Agents of the Secret Service must maintain the highest tiers of security while simultaneously respecting privacy, maintaining discretion and trust, and understanding that the organization's own public image coincides with one of the most powerful political figures in the world. It's an incredible burden, and one to which we all owe our gratitude. When it is spelled out with such simplicity, it is equally simple to understand why mistakes and missteps in security just cannot happen. It is also easy to understand what the agency's fundamental mission is: Protection. The average American on the street seems to know it, so one would think that the agency understands it, too. The highest order of the U.S. Secret Service is to keep the commander in chief safe. Anything else, to include image, is a moot point.

When the agency was founded in 1865, it was commissioned to regulate and stop the spread of counterfeit currency in a post–Civil War era. Only later did it take on the mandate that it is so well known for today; that of executive protection at the highest level. This later mission has remained its fundamental core competency ever since, and it is what sets the United States Secret Service apart from other federal law enforcement agencies. Although investigations have remained an intricate part of the career of a U.S. Secret Service Special Agent, the understanding is protection is why everyone is there.

But in the last few decades, the United States Secret Service has forgotten where it began and what it is. An agency that once defined itself by protecting people without negotiating how it will do it now does so with a wink-and-a-nod understanding that the criteria of protection is open to interpretation and adjustment. Someone in the agency came in one day and started replacing right and wrong with black and white, and incorrectly thought that the two meant the same thing.

The right thing is often the hard thing to do; if the right thing were easy, everyone would do the right thing all the time. And we know that doesn't happen. The organization that once told presidents where they could and could not go, decided one day to let White House staffers tell them how to secure a site for a visit, and it has never been the same; leaders who once did the right thing for their agents have been replaced with managers who buckle under the pressure of scheduling ridiculous hours of work for their subordinates, and the lack of morale and high attrition rate speaks for itself as the result. Field office agents who were once locked arm-in arm with their local law enforcement brethren on a protection assignment now tell their local counterparts to stand in corners, out of sight of the protectees who do not wish to see them. The leaders of yesteryear would have never tolerated such treatment of their law enforcement brothers, but the new and improved Secret

Service allows this to occur daily, and is blessed at the highest levels of its management offices to do so. The mission used to be protection but the new core competency in today's U.S. Secret Service is image. The agency has sacrificed its mission for its beauty.

For myself, joining the cadre of the United States Secret Service started twenty years before my first day on the job. As a young child, I had the privilege of having a friend whose father was an agent. My friend's father was a powerful, positive influence for me in my young life, and it was that influence that propelled my ambition to become a Secret Service Agent. All the professional choices in my life, to include military college, my service to my country as military officer, and just staying out of trouble in my youth were all a means to an end for me: That end was to become a U.S. Secret Service Agent.

The day that I received the call telling me that I was accepted into the agency was one of the happiest, proudest days of my life. I was home alone when the personnel office called, and I paced excitedly while I waited for my wife to come home from work to give her the news. When she arrived home and I told her, she leapt into my arms with an excited squeal. It was wonderful, exciting time for us both, filled with a promise for the future and assurance that I was about to be a part of something special and meaningful for my country; to be part of a great, honorable agency with a single mission focus.

I could not have been more disappointed when I arrived.

The very first thing I noticed was the lack of leadership and accountability amongst the agency. Supervisors were motivated by minute details on meaningless paperwork, and were quick to criticize young agents for ridiculous, subjective things. Abuses in authority were commonplace amongst managers, and morale was terribly low. Truly, the only thing I remember fondly about those days was the camaraderie and bonds I developed with my fellow "boot-agents." I genuinely miss the times with those people, and there were only a very limited few supervisors who earned my respect in those days. After nine years, I could take no more. I became another casualty to the problems, the cancer that infects the agency today.

From lack of quality management, to morale, to the hemorrhaging of personnel, the United States Secret Service is in dire need of major overhaul. With this being one of the most polarizing political atmospheres in our country's history, the demand for quality protection for our leaders is needed now more than ever, so the timing for the U.S. Secret Service to buckle under its own weight could not be worse.

When Dan told me that he was considering writing this book, I enthusiastically encouraged him to do so. Anyone who knows Dan Bongino tends to use words like character, integrity, and morality when describing him. In our time together as agents in the Baltimore Field Office, it was obvious Dan was a "right and wrong" kind of guy, and not a "black and white" one.

No one, professionally or personally, is better qualified to outline the problems that plague the United States Secret Service today; no one is better qualified to address the issues and offer the right answers to fix those problems.

As I read through Dan's book, I remembered the reasons why I joined the agency all those years ago, and also why I left. Although it is too late for me, the issues can still be corrected to make it an agency that future young men and women will dedicate their lives to joining and will proudly stay with for their careers; it's not too late for the U.S. Secret Service to return to its former glory. The road map to do that is in the pages before you, spelled out by the person who knows best how the agency can once again do the right things.

—JASON WELLS, U.S. SECRET SERVICE, 2005-2013
AUTHOR OF *OUR PATH TO SAFETY: A U.S. SECRET SERVICE AGENT'S GUIDE TO CREATING SAFE COMMUNITIES*

ACKNOWLEDGMENTS

The Secret Service will always be a part of me. They took a chance on me when they hired me as a special agent when I was a young New York City Police officer in my early twenties. I want to extend a sincere debt of gratitude to the working men and women of the Secret Service, who spend countless hours away from their wives, their husbands, their children, their homes, their beds, and their kitchen tables, all for the honor and distinction of sacrificing their lives first to save the life of the president of the United States. There is no nobler mission in federal law enforcement.

I want to thank my wife, Paula, for sticking by my side through the months spent on the road when I was a Secret Service agent, the weeks spent on the road when I was a candidate for public office, and the many days spent holed up in my office, preparing the material for this book. My wife never had it easy in her life. Her story of overcoming hardship on her road to becoming a citizen of this great country has always been a source of inspiration for me. Whenever I think I'm having a tough day, I center myself by remembering the struggles she went through as a child, and everything brightens up around me. I will never love another.

I want to thank my father, John, for always providing an example of what discipline and a commitment to hard work can accomplish, despite the long odds. He has always been the hardest-working man I know. Thank you to my mother-in-law as well for being the truest example I've seen of what the uniquely American dream looks like. She's an inspiration for me and my family.

I want to thank my two daughters, Isabel and Amelia, for filling a hole in my life. My life was all about me before my daughters were born, and lives lived that way are empty and devoid of real meaning. My daughters taught me what real purpose is, and what real love is.

I'd like to thank my brothers, Jim and Joseph, for hearing me out when I needed to vent; my friend and former coworker Brian for being that one true friend we all need; and Maria and Sharon for their advice, friendship, and guidance. Thanks to Senators Mike Lee, Rand Paul, and Ted Cruz for being authentic in a sea of DC counterfeits. Thanks to Congressmen Justin Amash and Louie Gohmert as well for your support in the tough times.

Thank you to Cary Katz for taking a chance on me and to the entire Conservative Review team for inspiring me to continue the fight for our collective principles, even as the obstacles in front of us mounted.

Finally, thank you to Mark Levin and Rich for always being there for me both personally and professionally, and thanks to Sean Hannity, Lynda, Lauren, and Jason for allowing me to be part of your radio family. No matter where I go, I'll always know where I began. And so will you.

LIST OF ACRONYMS

AOP	assault on principle
BATF	Bureau of Alcohol, Tobacco, Firearms and Explosives
CAT	Counter Assault Team
DHS	Department of Homeland Security
ECTF	Electronic Crimes Task Force
ESN	electronic serial number
FLD	First Lady's Detail
JJRTC	James J. Rowley Training Center
JOC	Joint Operations Center
LEAP	Law Enforcement Availability Pay
MED	Major Events Division (MED)
NSSE	National Special Security Events
OPFOR	opposition force
PDD-62	Presidential Decision Directive 62
PI	protective intelligence
PPD	Presidential Protective Division
ROTA	travel rotation
SAIC	Special Agent in Charge
VPPD	Vice Presidential Protective Division
WHMO	White House Medical Office

INTRODUCTION

I'VE HAD A LOT OF JOBS. I've stocked grocery shelves, delivered newspapers, patrolled crime-ridden streets as an NYPD police officer, consulted on business deals, hosted talk radio shows, hosted a successful podcast, and authored a couple of successful books. I've been a student many times, and a teacher a few times, but the position I'll always be proudest of is that of "Special Agent, United States Secret Service." Being a United States Secret Service agent is an awesome responsibility. A seasoned Secret Service agent knows how to be a cop, a diplomat, a peacemaker, a counselor, and a bodyguard (although I, and the agents I still call friends, hate that term when describing what the Secret Service does). The Secret Service is a relatively flat organization managerially, and as a result, they operate in a "sink or swim" environment where rank-and-file agents are given a significant amount of responsibility early on in their careers. It's not uncommon for a new special agent, only months or even days out of the Secret Service training academy, to be charged with designing an impenetrable security plan for a foreign head of state visiting the United States. During the annual United Nations General Assembly in New York City, tens to hundreds of foreign heads of state visit the United Nations in New York City, and they are all the responsibility of the United States Secret Service. But the Secret Service is, at best, a medium-sized federal agency that doesn't have the luxury of hundreds of thousands of experienced agents to cover every nook and cranny of New York City during the UN General Assembly. As a result, newer agents are forced, every year, to step up to the plate, early in their careers, and hit a security home run. There are no bunts allowed. Those agents who can handle the pressure of keeping the world's most powerful leaders secure will be the future leaders of the Presidential Protective Division (a Secret Service agents most coveted assignment), and of the Secret Service at large. Those who fail will be stuck investigating counterfeit currency cases out of a Secret Service field office to which no one wanted to be assigned, involving teenagers using mommy's color printer to create terrible-looking faux hundred-dollar bills, for the rest of their careers.

Being a Secret Service agent is a pressure cooker. But for those men and women who live for the rush of adrenaline that comes with fast motorcades, world travel, big responsibilities, and even bigger threats, it's the greatest job in the world. When I first joined the Secret Service in 1999 the agency was overflowing with applications, and when I made it through the arduous special agent selection process, I was genuinely surprised. Although I had faith in my abilities, I was convinced that my application was going to be swallowed up by the thousands of applications, from incredibly qualified men and women, the Secret Service was receiving for every special agent opening. I was honored to be a special agent, and the United States Secret Service "special agent" title instantly became part of me. The Secret Service was a proud, successful model government agency in 1999, and it reflected in the relatively high esprit de corps all the way from the upper management of the agency through the administrative staff.

In the early part of my nearly twelve-year career with the Secret Service, I was sent over to Moscow on a temporary investigative assignment. While there, I made friends with the FBI agent who also had an office at the American embassy in Moscow. During one of our many conversations, he was surprised to learn that the Secret Service allowed non-supervisory agents to conduct security advances for the president, vice president, and foreign heads of state. He was also surprised to learn that I was assigned as an instructor at the Secret Service training academy and that I was not a supervisor. He seemed particularly perplexed that I was assigned to the Russian embassy on a prestigious investigative assignment as nothing more than a GS-13 federal agent (Secret Service supervisors are all GS-14 and above). He told me that in the FBI most of the critical investigations, assignments, and FBI Academy instructor positions were filled either by senior special agents, or supervisors. The Secret Service doesn't work that way. Every special agent, whether a supervisor or not, is expected to be able to handle, on a moment's notice, an assignment where failure could mean the death of a world leader and a corresponding Archduke Ferdinand–like global crisis.

But the Secret Service is now living through an existential crisis. The overseas scandals, the fence jumpers, the Salahi incident, the stolen laptop, and other organizational black eyes on the agency have created a media, and political, feeding frenzy. Fair or unfair, media outlets smelled the blood in the water and saw the dollar signs from the click-bait headlines about the smallest Secret Service transgression, and they reported on every story no matter how thinly sourced. Some of these stories about the Secret Service were so misleading that the media outlets were forced to alter their headlines because the original reporting was not accurate. Remember the story about the Secret Service agents who "crashed a car into a White House barricade"?[1] Did you happen to notice the follow-up stories days after the original reporting, which described the exact same incident as Secret Service agents "nudging" a temporary orange traffic "barrier"?[2] Which one was it? Did the agents "crash" into a barrier, or did they "nudge" a traffic cone? One of these happened, and one clearly did not. The answer was obvious to anyone who viewed the security video of the incident, which was made public just days after it occurred. But it didn't matter; the media smelled blood, and they knew that using the word *crashed* to describe the incident, no matter how ridiculous and sensationalist, would generate eyeballs to their networks and clicks to their websites. It mattered little to these media figures that they destroyed the careers of the two agents involved in the incident, despite both of them having earned reputations as stellar performers and career-long team players. Lawmakers, themselves not immune to the smell of publicity blood in the water, jumped into the fray as well, and they have begun to question everything about the Secret Service, including its need to exist as a separate government agency. After the many crises the Secret Service has faced, a reasonable person would conclude that these incidents would serve as a wake-up call to the upper management of this once-great agency. But according to my many sources within the Secret Service, it's been largely business as usual, despite the withering media, legislative, and public pressure being put on the agency to evolve and improve.

That's why I decided to write this book. Although I feel strongly that the Secret Service has faced an unusual amount of unfair media coverage, the agency's problems are very real, and they require immediate action. The president of the United States is in genuine danger if the Secret Service doesn't change course soon and evolve with the rapidly changing threat environment. The threats to the White House and the president are swiftly evolving in this new era of weaponized drones, micro-sized video surveillance technology, vehicle attacks on civilians, small arms tactical assaults, and technologically advanced and difficult-to-detect explosives. And if the decision makers in the Secret

Service refuse to evolve with this series of threats, then, tragically, we may suffer the first loss of a president since John F. Kennedy. When I was a young Secret Service agent going through their special agent training program, the primary threats we trained to stop were single-shooter-type attacks, such as the attempted assassination of President Ronald Reagan. The response to an attack such as the Reagan shooting, and the corresponding training that accompanies it, are far different from the response to a weaponized drone flying directly into a presidential motorcade. The simplest example of this is weapons technology. The weapons most effective in suppressing a rapid-fire, single-person, handgun-based attack such as the Reagan shooting are not the same weapons that would be effective against an organized terrorist team's assault on the White House grounds using mortars, explosives, and automatic rifles.

I know many of you reading this book may be wondering, "Why give the bad guys any ideas by writing about security problems?" That's both a fair and an appropriate question, but I assure you, the "bad guys" already have these ideas, and worse, would carry them out tomorrow if the logistics involved with planning an attack on the White House were easier. But logistics can be figured out as long as the motivation to attack remains intact. And terrorism shows no signs of abating. Terrorist planners will find a way to acquire the technology, the weapons, the explosives, and the know-how to eventually make an attempt on the life of the president of the United States. The real question we should ALL be asking is, "What the hell are we going to do about it?"

PART 1

WHAT'S WRONG WITH THE SECRET SERVICE

1

THE SPECIAL AGENT MESS

WHEN LARGE ORGANIZATIONS EXPERIENCE SYSTEMIC FAILURES, these failures can be either top-down failures, driven by poor management decisions, or a bottom-up phenomenon, where the management's strategic plan was a good one, but the execution by the employees fails. Unfortunately, the special-agent side of the Secret Service has seen its share of both types of failures. But the critical problems facing the Secret Service special agent side today are primarily due to sclerotic management, obsessed with the "old way" of doing things. Secret Service headquarters–based upper management is dangerously risk-averse and nonresponsive to the evolving threat environment Secret Service special agents face. Combine this with the endless zeal by Secret Service management to expand the mission of the Secret Service, despite insufficient manpower and training to do so, and we have an agency on the verge of collapse.

When I joined the Secret Service in 1999, the dreaded Y2K crisis was on everyone's mind, and the agency had just completed a successful security operation for the visit of Pope John Paul II to the United States. Morale was universally high, and job complaints were few. Being a Secret Service agent in 1999 carried with it an unmistakable swagger. The agency had long since recovered from the multiple assassination attempts on Gerald Ford by Lynette "Squeaky" Fromme and Sara Jane Moore, and the shooting of Ronald Reagan by John Hinckley Jr., and the Secret Service was riding a successful, nearly two-decade-long streak of relatively scandal-free operations. The morning I reported for my first day on the job as an agent, I was seated in the small but professional-looking and well-maintained (which surprised me, given that I left the New York City Police Department to join the Secret Service, and the facilities were in atrocious condition) lobby of the Secret Service's New York field office, located in the pre–September 11, 2001, 7 World Trade Center building. I recall being impressed by the bravado and confidence of the agents who kept walking by. The New York field office had a swipe-card-and-PIN–based entry system at the time, and to get from one side of the office to the other, or one floor to the other, many of the agents would use the lobby as a shortcut. Every agent who entered the lobby would stop at the access control box, which would make a distinct beeping sound as each number of the agent's access PIN was entered. The scramble pad would scramble the digits on the keypad each time, so agents would have to bend over to look at the pad to see which keys to press. (This prevented any onlookers from detecting an agent's PIN when it was entered on the keypad.) As I sat in the lobby, both excited and anxious about my first day as a Secret Service agent, I noticed that every agent who passed me did the same thing. None of them looked at me directly, but instead they would bend over the scramble pad and, thinking I wasn't looking at them, tilt their heads to catch a glimpse at the new guy and then go on their way. Their collective glances at me all screamed the same thing: "This is the Secret Service. Are you ready?"

When I, and the other rookie agents I was hired with, were finally allowed into the office, with a special agent escort, I noticed the same confidence and swagger among the agents wandering the hallways. Everyone was talking about a big counterfeit arrest they had just made, a door they'd just knocked down on an arrest warrant, or how one of the New York field office agents had just gotten "picked up" by the "detail" (Secret Service jargon for being reassigned to the Presidential Protective Division). Adding icing to the swagger-cake, which all of the agents I ran into on my first day seemed to be eating, was our interaction with an agent headed out on a criminal search warrant. The agent, a solid two-hundred-plus pounds of muscle, wearing a "New York large" T-shirt (note: this is a standard medium-sized shirt, for the non-bodybuilder crowd across the fruited plains outside of New York City), paraded by with a battering ram breaching tool designed to forcibly take down a locked door while executing a search warrant. As he passed, he told us, in the loudest "inside voice" possible (note: this would be called screaming by a non–New Yorker), about the "perp" (short for perpetrator) they were going to lock up that day. If you were casting a movie about street-hardened New York Secret Service agents, you couldn't have had a more successful casting location than the hallways of the New York field office on my first day.

The whole scene was overwhelming, and impressive. And although everyone I ran into that day had an unmistakable swagger and confidence, it wasn't misplaced or rude. For me, a young twentysomething who had only known about the Secret Service through Hollywood movies and fiction books but had always idolized the Secret Service and their awesome mission, this air of self-assurance was simply the fulfilling of my high expectations. It would be no different from walking into the

New York Yankees' locker room after a World Series winning season and noticing that same swagger. You would probably be disappointed if you entered the Yankees' locker room under these circumstances and saw the team with hanging heads, their shoulders hunched, bitching and moaning about how terrible it was to be a Yankee. Thankfully, that was not the case in the New York field office, and it was clear to me that these seasoned agents were proud of their chosen profession and knew how to "win."

Athletes and coaches talk about learning how to win all the time, and it's an indispensable part of a successful organization. Aaron Rodgers, the Super Bowl–winning MVP quarterback for the Green Bay Packers, once told the sports media before a playoff game, "I think you have to learn how to win in the playoffs."[1] Notice, Rodgers didn't say, "I think you have to learn how to *play* in the playoffs." He specifically said, ". . . learn how to *win*." Learning to win is a longitudinal exercise in repeated, successful execution that imbues an organization with an attitudinal productivity factor not explainable by the sum of individual efforts. Being on a "winning" team is the X factor teams and coaches have been trying to bottle, and re-create, throughout the history of human competition in both sports and business. But sometimes having the best players, or the brightest employees, doesn't translate into learning how to win (just ask the 2004 USA basketball team, which finished with a disappointing bronze Olympic medal despite having a team composed of elite NBA All-Stars). In 1999, the Secret Service was an organization that knew exactly how to win.

At some point between the closing years of the Bill Clinton presidency and the Secret Service transfer from the Department of the Treasury to the Department of Homeland Security (DHS) in 2003, the Secret Service stopped winning. As special agents during this 2003 transfer, many of us were unsure about how it was going to impact the mission, or us personally, in the future. But the actual transfer was relatively uneventful. We all received shiny new badges and identification cards, but other than those cards reading, "Department of Homeland

Security" rather than "The Department of the Treasury," and the badges getting bigger and shinier (the new DHS badges added a large, silver, five-pointed star overlay on top of a new gold badge), nothing really changed in the short term. Our paychecks were still direct-deposited in our bank accounts in the same amounts, and the paperwork to conduct criminal investigations, security advances, to inventory evidence, and to account for our man-hours, despite desperately needing revision, all remained unchanged. Even our offices stayed in the same locations as they were before the transfer. I, along with many agent colleagues of mine, pondering the nonevent of the transfer, began to wonder after a few months what the point of the transfer to DHS was. If consolidation and efficiency improvements through the leveraging of economies of scale and scope weren't the goals of the transfer, and nothing really changed on the ground, then why did the politicians and bureaucratic class make this move? Looking back on the decision through the lens of the post–September 11, 2001, world, it appears that the decision was a reactionary political "solution" looking for a problem to solve. The Secret Service was "winning," and performing admirably, under the Treasury Department and, ironically, doing so using half of the roughly two billion federal tax dollars it currently consumes.

IF YOU ASKED A HANDFUL OF SENIOR SECRET SERVICE AGENTS why the Secret Service stopped winning during the period in question, you would get an assortment of different answers, but many of those answers would include the infamous DHS transfer, poor management, a broken pay scale, a broken promotion system, and the expanding mission of the Secret Service that immediately preceded the DHS transfer. Many of the agents in my cohort called the DHS transfer the "hostile takeover" and saw almost nothing positive come from it, while simultaneously noting that the "winning" stopped after the transfer. In my experience, most of the special agent mess that occurred immediately before and pursuant to the DHS transfer can be attributed to the significant "mission creep" that occurred within the Secret Service during those years. When the Secret

Service was located within the Treasury Department, they had limited criminal investigative duties, and their tacitly understood (because Secret Service management couldn't acknowledge formally that their criminal investigations were often sidelined in lieu of protection missions or they would run the risk of losing the investigative functions altogether) primary function was protection. To the rank-and-file special agents, this was always understood to mean that whatever criminal case you were working on at the time, whether it was a counterfeit currency case or a credit-card fraud case, the investigation was going to take a backseat if a Secret Service protectee came into your district. We all knew that we were expected to drop everything when the president, vice president, their families, or a foreign head of state planned to visit our assigned areas of responsibility. This drop-everything-for-protection agency mind-set caused a lot of headaches with the local assistant United States attorneys (the government prosecutors assigned to prosecute federal investigations through the federal legal system) because if an agent was assigned to a case where a federal arrest had been made, and the prosecution phase had begun, the assistant U.S. attorneys would have to constantly juggle around the court schedule based on the ability of the Secret Service agents to appear. (Federal judges weren't big fans of this either and wouldn't hesitate to let us know through the assistant U.S. attorneys.)

This "drop everything" for protection approach to federal investigations hit close to home with me during the prosecution phase of multimillion-dollar credit card fraud ring I was investigating in 2000 and 2001. The suspects in the case had unlocked a proprietary algorithm that credit card companies used to create account numbers, and they were probing the numbers with small, nearly unnoticeable purchases to determine which credit card numbers were active. When they found an active card number, they would create a counterfeit credit card bearing the stolen account number, and then proceed to local chain stores to buy gift cards. They would sell the gift cards for cash, at a discount, later. The scam was enormous in size and scope. Hundreds of millions of dollars were lost to fraud in this scam, and it was suspected that a portion of the ill-gotten gains was being used to finance international terror groups. We broke up the scheme, after months of painstaking surveillance and investigative forensics, when we caught a low-level operator in the scheme on camera using one of the counterfeit credit cards in a hardware store. With a criminal case of this magnitude, a casual observer would think that the Secret Service would prioritize the investigation, but unfortunately, that wasn't the case. The Secret Service is a protection-centric agency, and Hillary Clinton was running for the U.S. Senate seat in New York at the time. Due to the competitive nature of the race, Mrs. Clinton became a frequent visitor to Long Island, the area of New York I was assigned to cover. Each visit by Mrs. Clinton delayed the investigation and prosecution of the credit card fraud case, as I was pulled off the case to do security advances and protection assignments. The size of the fraud case (based on the incredible volume of credit card numbers stolen), combined with the mounting financial losses in the hundreds of millions, made the workload for the case suffocating given my expanding protective responsibilities with Mrs. Clinton. (Thankfully, I worked the case with an understanding FBI agent who would fill in for me when I had to cancel a court appearance or an appointment with the assistant U.S. attorney.) I learned to forget about weekends because the week never actually ended. I would go from a criminal surveillance related to the fraud case, to protection, to court, and then repeat the cycle the next week. I spent weekends either on protection or formulating reports on the fraud case. Still, although it was a headache balancing the dual protection and investigative missions of the Secret Service, it was manageable outside of campaign season. (The Hillary Clinton protection workload was an exception because the Long Island Secret Service office to which I was assigned only had a few working agents assigned to it, unlike the New York field office, which had hundreds of special agents assigned there.) The assistant U.S. attorneys gave us a lot of slack (it didn't hurt that we would get them pictures with the Secret Service protectees if they asked).

It was right around this busy time in my nascent Secret Service career that the Secret Service's dual mission started transforming into the never-ending mission. The agents were still adjusting to the dramatic increase in protection assignments because of the unprecedented situation that had developed with Hillary Clinton. Secret Service agents had historically had a light travel schedule when they were assigned to the First Lady's Detail (FLD), but Mrs. Clinton's decision to run for the U.S. Senate in New York changed all of that. Her schedule mutated into a campaign schedule, not a First Lady's schedule, which largely consisted of ceremonial events in the past. And although morale was still strong, despite the onslaught of protective assignments emanating from the Presidential Protective Division's Operations Section (responsible for handling the logistics for the First Lady's travel), I began to hear grumblings from agents about the relentless protection workload. Unfortunately, the growing portfolio of protection assignments due to Mrs. Clinton's campaign for office happened not long after the Secret Service took on the lead role for securing nationally significant events determined to be "National Special Security Events" (NSSE) in 2000 pursuant to the Presidential Decision Directive 62 (PDD-62)[2] and the Presidential Threat Protection Act of 2000.[3]

Initially, the Secret Service's new role in securing NSSE events was limited by the infrequency of the designation. Before the DHS transfer it was relatively uncommon for an event to be designated an NSSE, and as a result, the detailed planning and manpower requirements needed from the Secret Service to secure these NSSE events were limited. But after the DHS transfer, these events became more regular, as seemingly every national summit or sports event tried to pass off their security costs to the federal government by obtaining an NSSE designation and having the Secret Service pick up the security tab. These NSSE events—from the Salt Lake City, Utah, Winter Olympics, to the Sea Island, Georgia, G-8 summit—were all vacuums sucking up Secret Service manpower and forcing agents into unmanageable professional lives, and even more stressful personal lives. As a result of the growing demand for its security services through the NSSE designation, the Secret Service expanded and started a new division to handle NSSE events. The new division was called the Major Events Division (MED), and as with every new government creation, this division has to be staffed with Secret Service agent personnel, with a fresh influx of taxpayer dollars to the agency to pay for it. The MED and the NSSE designation began a few years before the transfer to DHS, but in the eyes of many of the agents working through the DHS transfer, the correlation between the mission creep of the Secret Service and their deteriorating home lives and unmanageable work schedules left an indelible mark. And the DHS transfer became a convenient source of blame and agency scorn.

Pursuant to the Secret Service's new NSSE responsibilities as national "event planners," special agents were now being asked to act as elite protection agents for the world's most threatened men and women, to function as tier-one financial crimes criminal investigators, and, as a result of the NSSE designation, to function as security guards for events with a lobbying staff big enough, or connected to enough of the "right people," to obtain an NSSE designation. This is a story about the fall of the Secret Service that is rarely told in the media, but I lived it, and the complaints started to pile up as the NSSE events did. One of the complaints I heard often in the early 2000s, as the Secret Service was expanding at an uncontrollable rate, was "I didn't sign up to be a security guard for a bunch of connected insiders." Keep in mind, many of these men and women signed up to be Secret Service special agents aspiring to protect the president of the United States, but the NSSE designation meant that many of these agents were securing events that the president didn't even necessarily attend. Skipping a few court dates on a big criminal investigation to protect the First Lady, the president, or a foreign head of state was what most of the agents understood as their calling, not watching a door for twelve hours outside of some international summit of self-important international wannabe big shots. The hit to special agent morale was devastating.

UNFORTUNATELY, THE SECRET SERVICE MISSION CREEP didn't end with the expansion into NSSE events and the founding of the Major Events Division. In the late '90s and early 2000s, the New York field office started informally investigating cellular phone fraud occurring within New York City. No one in Congress, the Treasury Department, or the Department of Homeland Security told the Secret Service to do these investigations; the New York field office was simply responding to a barrage of complaints about "cloned" cellular phones and the subsequent requests from the cell phone industry to do something about it. The "cloning" of cell phones was an enormous problem for both the cellular phone industry and their customers during the late 1990s and early 2000s, and it was doing real damage to consumer confidence in the burgeoning industry. Every cell phone has an electronic serial number (ESN) in addition to the phone number, and technologically savvy thieves were using radio frequency interception devices to steal the phone number and the ESN combinations from cell phone owners and "cloning" them onto other cell phone devices. This enabled the thieves to sell "cloned" cellular phones, which would then be billed to the legitimate owner of the phone with the authentic ESN/phone number combination. Seeking help with this problem, representatives from some of the major cell phone service providers, who had worked previously with members of the Secret Service's New York field office on financial crimes cases, began to work with their special agent contacts on investigating and prosecuting the cell phone fraudsters. Seems harmless enough, right? Well, it wasn't. As agents from the New York field office investigated increasing numbers of these cases, the Secret Service's investigative mission began to expand correspondingly. The investigative mission at that time was clear: the Secret Service was charged with investigating counterfeit U.S. currency, and financial crimes, such as check-kiting, bank fraud, credit card fraud, and U.S. Treasury check fraud. The Secret Service was not set up in the late 1990s to be an agency responsible for the investigation of electronic crimes such as cellular phone cloning. Yet, this is exactly what happened. The Secret Service and its headquarters management got starry-eyed seeing the potential gusher of post-retirement jobs in lucrative technology fields, such as the cellular phone industry. Add to that the pressure from a group of mid-level Secret Service managers in the New York field office and—voilá! The Secret Service became an electronic crimes investigative outfit as well as a protection agency, national "event planners," and a financial crimes outfit. It happened. I was there.

At this point, you may be asking, "Was there an act of Congress, based on some study of Secret Service capabilities to take on this mammoth investigative responsibility in the electronic crimes sphere, that led to the Secret Service becoming the federal law enforcement agency responsible for leading the federal electronic crimes task forces?" Unfortunately, no, there wasn't. The Secret Service's humble electronic crimes beginnings, investigating cell phone cloning, rapidly evolved into one of the largest cases of federal law enforcement mission creep in modern history as the investigation of cell phone fraudsters morphed into the New York field office's Electronic Crimes Task Force (ECTF). Led by a charismatic first-level supervisor at the time whom I'll call Bill, the New York field office ECTF began to expand its tentacles into computer crimes, Internet child pornography, unauthorized movie and music trading over the Internet, and, critically, the trading of stolen credit card information over the Internet. Bill was a smooth operator with a Rolodex of contacts that would make the phone book jealous, and he rapidly expanded the mission of the New York field office ECTF and, by proxy, the Secret Service. He almost single-handedly expanded the mission of the Secret Service by contacting technology leaders and offering to work with them in the investigation and prosecution of criminals exploiting the still relatively new Internet for criminal purposes. Bill was a hardworking and dedicated agent, and I am in no way attempting to impugn his character by writing about his efforts to stem the growing menace of Internet-based crimes, but as with many good intentions within government, the real-world results of this new and expanded Secret Service mission was an expansion of the Secret

Service mission not commensurate with its experience, manpower, or equipment capabilities. This further damaged special agent morale as the agency workload continued to expand unabated.

The impact of this dramatic expansion of the Secret Service's traditional, statutory investigative role, and into the electronic crimes arena, impacted me personally, and many of the other members of the special agent workforce in 2003 and 2004. The origins of the dramatic drop in Secret Service morale within the New York field office, based on my many conversations with agents working in the office at the time, can be traced to this time period due to the New York Office ECTF's investigation of "Shadowcrew," a fraud case later made famous when it was featured on CNBC's popular television show *American Greed*. This large, and nearly unmanageable, Secret Service electronic crimes case, dubbed "Operation Firewall" by the agency, was, in the eyes of many of the Secret Service's headquarters managers, their way to show the world what the Secret Service could do in the electronic crimes arena. Operation Firewall was a complicated, international investigation where an organized group of technologically sophisticated thieves traded in large numbers of stolen credit card numbers over websites they monitored and managed. One of the Secret Service's key informants in the case, a man named Albert Gonzalez, was to provide a window into the operations of the websites trafficking in these stolen credit card numbers. Gonzalez later made a fool of the agency when it was discovered that during the course of his informant work for the New York ECTF, he was also committing additional Internet-based crimes by hacking into corporate networks to steal more credit card information.

Operation Firewall could have appropriately been called "Operation Chaos" within the Secret Service's New York field office because chaos is exactly what this case caused. The Secret Service's dual investigative mission was becoming unmanageable as the 1990s ended and the new millennium began. The use of Secret Service agent manpower to plan for and secure NSSE events, the corresponding staffing of the new Secret Service "Major Events Division," the expanding portfolio of people under Secret Service protection after the 9/11 terror attacks, and the new electronic crimes investigative mission strained the agency to the point of bursting. When the George W. Bush reelection effort, and the corresponding presidential election campaign season, began in 2003, agency morale soured across the country. I was assigned to a satellite office of the New York field office at the time, based on Long Island, and I recall a steady stream of complaints from agents forced to spend months on the road supporting presidential travel for the campaign, while many of the Operation Firewall agents were "hands-off." "Hands-off" was Secret Service manpower jargon for agents taken off of the protection travel rotation, known as the ROTA (short for rotation). To ensure that agent travel from the Secret Service field offices around the country, and the world, in support of the protection mission of the agency, was equitably distributed among its international workforce, the Secret Service developed the ROTA to prevent agents from burning out on the road. Traveling for protection assignments in the Secret Service wasn't much of a hardship when I was a young agent, full of vigor and eager to see the world. But after years spent on the road, and after marriage and children, I, along with most of my agent coworkers who had families, found travel to be incredibly tedious and we all looked forward to our own beds, time with our families, and home-cooked meals. Operation Firewall screwed up the ROTA for agents all across the country because the size of the investigation had vacuumed up dozens of agents, across multiple field offices, who were all pulled off the ROTA to support the Operation Firewall investigation. The complexity of the Operation Firewall case only stoked the flames of division within the Secret Service because many of the agents, forced to spend additional weeks on the road in protection assignments because of the shrunken ROTA, didn't even understand what the hell the case was about and why the Secret Service was even involved in electronic crime.

Put yourself in the shoes of a married agent, with children, during this period, trying to explain to a wife working her own eight-hour day while also driving the kids to school, preparing their lunches, bathing them, and soothing crying young ones, that you're on the road for an additional three weeks because of an electronic crime case being run out of the New York field office ECTF. Understandably, many of the spouses were pissed off, and they let their special agent husbands and wives know about it. Many of the spouses had been with their agent husbands and wives through the early 1990s, and they remembered protective travel assignments, but few could recall their husbands or wives being endlessly on the road. Compounding matters, and aggravating the souring morale among agents outside of the "hands-off" Operation Firewall, was the arrogant attitude some of the agents involved in the investigation of the case displayed toward the many of us in the New York field office and its satellite offices who were managing our own complex criminal investigations while *also* traveling around the globe to support protection missions. "Why am I canceling court dates and putting *my* investigations on hold to support the Operation Firewall agents?" we asked.

One of the ironic, and lasting, consequences of the Operation Firewall investigation wasn't just its role in damaging morale and causing a spike in attrition as many New York agents simply left the job when work conditions deteriorated. The mishandling of the case was also damaging to the Secret Service's investigative reputation. This is troubling because the gravity of the case, as measured by the catastrophic losses to the credit card industry and the unprecedented use of the "dark web," presented a real opportunity for the Secret Service to shine when it broke up this major, international fraud ring. But it wound up having the opposite effect. The Secret Service entered the electronic crime sector through its early work on cell phone fraud cases and the industry contacts "Bill" had developed working these cases. It expanded, largely without the training and expertise to do so, into the Internet crimes sector and immediately plunged itself into the enormous Operation Firewall investigation. New York field office ECTF agents then broke the case by turning a member of the criminal organization running the fraud scheme into a paid federal law enforcement informant.

This informant, hired as a government cooperator, then turned on the Secret Service and used his vastly superior computer knowledge (given the Secret Service's lack of training and expertise in electronic crimes at the time) to commit additional crimes while, astonishingly, on the government payroll. The agents investigating this case were then pulled off of the travel ROTA, forcing the government to pay extra taxpayer dollars in overtime to overworked Secret Service agents forced to stay on the road and remain on the ROTA to cover for the agents monitoring the informant who was screwing over the Secret Service. This series of unfortunate events further damaged Secret Service agent morale and subsequently led to a spike in resignations. The disastrous handling of the case was a source of more fuel for the brewing discontent and worsening morale within the once-proud agency. In addition, many of the Operation Firewall agents, with their favorable work schedules due to their roles in the investigation, had availed themselves of some of the best contacts the technology industry offered as a result of being assigned to the ECTF. They then used these contacts to leave the Secret Service and take lucrative positions within many of the companies that were part of the Operation Firewall investigation or working with the ECTF. It's an almost unbelievable story until you realize that it's the federal government at the heart of it. Only the government can manage screwups like this with virtually no long-term accountability.

The federal law enforcement bureaucracy has countless stories like this, which provides additional evidence pointing to an aimless law enforcement alphabet soup of federal agencies, with no credible long-term plan, that delegates both de facto and statutory investigative authority to federal law enforcement agencies based on "connections," parochial desires, and accidents of history. Ironically, even the Secret Service's role as a protection agency came about, not as a result of a detailed plan based on the Secret Service's capabilities and expertise, but because of public pressure to protect our presidents after the assassination of President William McKinley in September 1901. The Secret Service was informally protecting McKinley's successor, Vice President

Theodore Roosevelt, after McKinley's assassination, but they only became formally responsible for this mission years later, in 1906. The Secret Service was founded in 1865 not to protect the president, but to investigate the growing stock of counterfeit currency in the United States. Protecting the president is not a mission that requires the same set of skills necessary to conduct complex financial crimes investigations. Yet, similar to its usurpation of investigative responsibilities in the electronic crimes arena, it took over as the nation's premier personal protection agency based on proximity to power, and an accident of history.

The Secret Service's lead federal law enforcement role in the investigation of electronic crimes is now formal, despite its inability to manage its pre-electronic crimes investigative and protection missions. The 2001 PATRIOT Act, signed into law by President George W. Bush, cemented into law the Secret Service's role as the lead agency responsible for the coordination of the nation's electronic crimes task forces. And though this expansion has greatly widened the window of opportunity for postretirement employment for Secret Service agents, and for current agents with electronic crimes experience looking to escape the federal government for the more lucrative confines of the technology industry, it has been a disaster for Secret Service morale. This quote from a 2015 *Washington Post* piece sums up the catastrophic Secret Service morale problem: "The Secret Service ranks 319 out of 320 agencies, with a 'sizable drop in employee satisfaction in all 10 workplace categories.' The agency's current index score measuring employee engagement is at a new low, 28 percent lower than last year and just half what it was 10 years ago."[4] With the exception of one worse-off agency, number 320 out of 320 on the agency morale scale, it literally couldn't get any worse for the Secret Service.

IN MY EXPERIENCE AS A SECRET SERVICE AGENT from 1999 through 2011, mission creep was a significant factor in the destruction of Secret Service special agent morale. But it wasn't the only factor. The Secret Service also had a problem with unresponsive management during this same time period. The management became infamous among the working agents on the protective details, and in the field offices, for answering nearly every critical question about systemic problems within the Secret Service with "Because that's the way we've always done it." The 2014 United States Secret Service Protective Mission Panel's report, which analyzed problems within the Secret Service, clearly fingered this problem by stating, "The Panel found an organization starved for leadership that rewards innovation and excellence and demands accountability. From agents to officers to supervisors, we heard a common desire: More resources would help, but what we really need is leadership."[5]

Secret Service leadership failed the agents on multiple fronts during my tenure with the agency, but one specific management-caused problem was particularly damaging to morale during this period. In the decades before I entered the Secret Service in 1999, it wasn't uncommon for a Secret Service agent to relocate multiple times in his or her career. This need to constantly move agents around the country was due to the agency's protection requirements, which were largely based out of Washington, DC, where both the Presidential and Vice Presidential Protective divisions (PPD and VPPD, respectively) were located. If you were an agent hired to work out of an office in Montana, then the standard career path for you would be approximately five to eight years in Montana; a transfer to either the PPD or VPPD in Washington, DC; a transfer to a second Washington, DC–based assignment; and then a transfer back to a field office outside of Washington, DC. If you were actively seeking a promotion, then you would have to relocate again, most likely back to Washington, DC, to fill an open supervisory position either at the Secret Service headquarters or on the PPD or VPPD. In the tighter job markets of the early 1990s, this was a small price to pay for the stability of a high-paying and well-respected job as a Secret Service agent. But as the late 1990s technology economy took off, and as the post–September 11, 2001, federal law enforcement hiring boom followed, it made little sense to remain in a job where you were expected to uproot your family and move every few years when you could earn the same amount of money, or more, in another federal law enforcement position, or the private sector.

There were few policies in the Secret Service despised more than the informal "you have to take a move" policy. Adding insult to injury, many of the headquarters-based managers who had the power to fix these problems instead dismissed the concerns of a growing body of agents who were rapidly tiring of endless travel in support of the protection mission and the pressure to constantly relocate to places where they had no roots. Yet, despite the changing job conditions in the economy at large, and the dramatic post 9/11 uptick in hiring among other federal law enforcement agencies that had no such relocation requirement, the Secret Service management refused to change the informal relocation policy, while making only token changes to the "career track" options for agents. In an effort to stem the growing tide of discontent surrounding the extensive protection-related travel, and the unnecessary relocation requirement, Secret Service management introduced new career tracks intended to allow special agents to stay in one field office and avoid relocating their families. But although agents were now eligible for a new "investigative career track" (created in response to the attrition problem resulting from the relocation requirement), enabling them to stay in their original field office for an extended period of time, management never took the career track seriously. Agents who chose the new investigative career track quickly figured out that it was a raw deal in two respects. First, many of the agents who chose the new career track in order to spend more time with their families and avoid relocating to new homes in far-away places, often found their families alone anyway, as the agents were still being bombarded with ROTA protection assignments on the road. Second, most of the agents who chose not to relocate in favor of the new investigative career track were locked out of promotion assignments because they never served on a protection detail and were subsequently ineligible to bid for promotion on supervisory positions on those protective details. Combine this with the inescapable reality within the Secret Service that the culture was one that valued service on a full-time protection detail (agents who never served in these protective assignments were viewed as second-class citizens), and the pressure to relocate and join a protective detail, or to find another job in federal law enforcement, became overwhelming. The Secret Service could have solved this problem, and the NSSE problem, and the ECTF problem, and the never-ending mission creep problem, by simply stating the obvious: the Secret Service had outgrown their investigative mission. By focusing exclusively on the protection mission, and abandoning portions of the investigative mission no longer suited to their workforce capacities, the Secret Service would only have to relocate a special agent once, when the agent was hired.

The relocation requirement for special agents was a hammer to agent morale that the Secret Service still has not recovered from. And the failure to change this organizational relic, or to streamline the Secret Service's mission, is the fault of Secret Service management who seemingly cannot see the forest for the trees. But another morale killer in the Secret Service, which is not the fault of Secret Service management, is the salary cap imposed upon its special agents. The Secret Service is one of the few federal law enforcement agencies that pays overtime. Most federal law enforcement agents have overtime pay built into their regular paychecks through a program called LEAP (Law Enforcement Availability Pay), where the agent's salary requirements are covered by an annual salary plus an additional 25 percent of his or her salary to cover anticipated overtime hours. LEAP largely covers the additional overtime hours federal law enforcement agents routinely work, in addition to their eight-hour workdays, to compensate the agents for such things as after-hours surveillance operations, arrests, and other investigative operational requirements that wouldn't ordinarily fit into a standard eight-hour workday. As a result, most federal agencies don't routinely pay additional overtime, outside of LEAP, because it's rare for their agents to work more than the 25 percent LEAP supplement included in their pay package. This is not the case with Secret Service agents. The investigative, and protection-related, mission creep, and the relocation requirements, caused an attrition death spiral beginning in the early 2000s that continues through today. As the special agent workforce shrunk, not in nominal terms but relative to the expanding Secret Service mission, and the hiring of new agents struggled to keep pace, the remaining agents were forced to pick up additional ROTA assignments, which resulted in millions of dollars in additional overtime costs accrued as a result of having to pay a smaller cadre of agents for more hours worked. The mission requirements of the Secret Service are clear; when a security plan calls for thirty agents to stand post at a rally site for a Secret Service protectee, then the Secret Service is going to find exactly thirty agents to fulfill the mission. They don't really care how long you've been on the road or how tired you are if you're one of the agents assigned the task. Working without days off, and traveling from state to state with little sleep, in support of the protection mission is tedious enough, but doing it for no additional compensation has been devastating to the agent workforce. Secret Service agent compensation, along with other federal agent pay, is legislatively capped at approximately $160,000 per year, and in busy election seasons, which now run up to two years long, it is not uncommon for agents to max out their overtime pay by April or May. (Note: the federal fiscal year used for budgeting, and to calculate compensation, runs from October to the end of September, not January to the end of December.) Once an agent is "maxed out" (Secret Service jargon for earning the maximum amount of money allowable under the salary cap), then that agent cannot earn any more overtime pay, and any hours worked and accumulated after his or her forty-hour workweek, plus the agent's ten hours of LEAP per week, are uncompensated.

I fully understand how many of you reading this would question why this is such a big deal. After all, $160,000 per year is a lot of money. Yes, you are correct: that is a lot of money for a position within the federal government, and no Secret Service agent I know would dispute that. But it's not the amount of money that most of the agents have a problem with; it's the structure of their pay relative to other federal law enforcement agencies that has damaged Secret Service morale. Here's a simple test: would you remain in a job that asks you to work seventy-plus hours a week for the same salary as a similar job requiring only fifty hours a week? My guess is you probably wouldn't. Many agents stay behind because they love the mission of the Secret Service and they love their country, but many are leaving to take positions with the BATF, the IRS, the DEA, the FBI, and other agencies, because they, and their families, are simply burned-out from spending close to a decade of their lives on the road. I remember having a conversation with a former Secret Service agent who had resigned to take a position with another federal law enforcement agency. He told me that his boss's desk was littered with applications and résumés from Secret Service agents looking to leave the Secret Service and join his agency. It was depressing to hear. No one wants to be part of an agency where they feel as though they're going to be the last one to turn the lights out as everyone leaves.

The Secret Service cannot effectively protect the president in the future with its current portfolio of problems. Mission creep has saddled the Secret Service with an expanded plate of responsibilities that it no longer has the manpower, budget, or training to effectively handle. Poor management decisions, made with the best interests of upper-level Secret Service management but the worst interests of the working agents in the field in mind, have also ravaged the workforce and destroyed both special agent morale, and faith in the leadership. When combined with a special agent pay scale that incentivizes Secret Service agents to seek employment elsewhere within the federal law enforcement alphabet soup of agencies, it's no surprise that failures have begun to pile up within the Secret Service. No organization, whether public or private, can be expected to perform at an elite level, and with zero operational errors, while simultaneously losing their best employees and saddling those who remain with hostility toward the organization and its leadership.

2

THE UNIFORMED DIVISION OFFICER MESS

ALL TOO OFTEN, WHEN I read media reports about newsworthy events involving the Secret Service, the reporter incorrectly identifies the Secret Service personnel involved. The Secret Service as currently constituted has two separate entities with different, albeit slightly overlapping, functions. The Secret Service special agent side of the agency is responsible for the protection of the president of the United States. The special agents follow the president around both on and off the White House grounds. They are the "body men." They surround and protect the human body elected to the office of the U.S. presidency. You've likely seen the special agent side of the Secret Service as portrayed in popular culture in movies such as *In the Line of Fire*, starring Clint Eastwood and, on the criminal-investigative side, as portrayed in movies such as *To Live and Die in L.A.*, starring William Petersen. Secret Service special agents do not wear uniforms, and they are most often dressed in suits and ties with their weapons, ammunition, communications gear, handcuffs, and flashlights concealed underneath their suit jackets. They are recognizable by their lapel pins, which change often for security measures, and their iconic earpieces. The earpiece has become so tied to the image of the Secret Service special agent that I often heard White House staffers speak of "earpiece envy," their desire for an earpiece-wearing security detail of their own because of the impressive visual that creates. Having served on the special agent side of the Secret Service, and having protected many of these high-ranking executive branch personnel, I always found this to be a curious phenomenon. After a few months of having a full-time Secret Service protective detail, most of the people I protected, outside of the president, found it slightly embarrassing being followed around constantly by burly special agents in suits and earpieces. I recall an incident with one protectee who was trying to get a haircut on a weekend in suburban Maryland. Horrified at the thought of a couple of guys in suits standing over the barber during the haircut, the protectee preferred that we wait outside of the barber shop.

Ironically, the earpiece as a distinguishing mark of who is, and who isn't, a Secret Service agent brings with it some comedy. While working a presidential daughter's detail in Northern California with an agent friend of mine, the earpiece, or lack thereof, actually saved us from being outed as agents. I was holding the cars that day (an agent always stays with the vehicles to ensure the quick availability of an escape option and to prevent an adversary from planting a listening device or explosive on the car), and my partner for the day walked back to the car with the protectee and starting laughing. I asked him what was so funny and he said he had been in a high-end shoe store with the protectee when two women thought they recognized her and began to loudly wonder whether that was her or a doppelganger. The women went back and forth for a moment saying "Is it her?" before settling on the fact that it couldn't be her because there were no Secret Service agents around. How did they come to that conclusion? One woman told the other, "We would see their Secret Service earpieces."

The earpiece marker has also led to some uncomfortable moments with low-level White House staff members during my career. In my early days on the Presidential Protective Division, I was assigned to an overseas trip with President George W. Bush, and one of the White House staffers we were working with got himself caught up in a small imbroglio surrounding an earpiece. A lesson I learned early on in my tenure as a Secret Service agent is that in many formerly Communist and authoritarian countries, the people that make the decisions for the foreign government hold the gun carriers in high esteem. As one military/security representative (sometimes it's difficult to appropriately distinguish between these two roles in countries with a history of authoritarian rule) once told me, "He who has the guns, has the power." The low-level White House staffer on the trip learned this lesson early in the visit, and every time he was asked by a host-government representative, not familiar with the staff/Secret Service breakdown, if he was a Secret Service agent, he would say "I'm with the Secret Service." Now, technically, he wasn't lying. He was "with the Secret Service" but he wasn't actually *with* the Secret Service. But he had a radio and an earpiece, and he needed to get things done, and he knew that the host-government would likely ignore him if they knew he was a low-level staff member (with no gun), so he kept up the charade of being "with the Secret Service" for days.

The charade came to a halt when a host-government representative approached me and told me he was going to move a piece of equipment because the "Secret Service agent told me to." I asked him which agent had told him that and he pointed to the White House staff member. I'd had enough at this point (this staff member and I had some history), and although it was going to be uncomfortable because I really didn't want to embarrass the poor guy, I called him over and asked him point-blank,

"Did you tell this guy you were a Secret Service agent?" He started to sweat and I knew he was cornered. I asked the host-government official to leave to avoid further embarrassing the staffer, but I wasn't going to let it go without letting him know the gravity of what he did. Impersonating a federal agent is a crime, I told him (granted, calling this particular incident a "crime" was probably a stretch, but this staffer was causing some problems on the trip and needed a stern warning), and I warned him that if he did it again it was going "up the chain" (Secret Service lingo for getting White House and Secret Service management involved). The staffer kept the earpiece in his ear after that but, thankfully, dropped the "I'm with the Secret Service" act.

The other side of the Secret Service, not immediately recognizable by the suits-and-earpiece combination (although they have earpieces too), is the Uniformed Division. Uniformed Division personnel are not agents; they are federal police officers, and they are recognizable by their black-and-white, police-style uniforms. Most Uniformed Division officers wear a standard white, button-down, collared shirt with the presidential seal on the left shoulder and a black tie in the winter and fall months. Due to the oppressive Washington, DC, heat, they wear white short-sleeve shirts with no tie in the spring and summer months. Their pants are black and otherwise indistinct. The Secret Service Uniformed Division uniform was routinely mocked, oftentimes by the officers themselves. A few of my agent friends who had transferred to the special agent side from the Uniformed Division told me they hated the uniform and that they used to derisively call it the "Black Knights of the Potomac" uniform.

The Uniformed Division is separate and distinct from the agent side of the Secret Service, and although they fall under the collective Secret Service agency umbrella, they have separate functions, job categories, and job descriptions. Secret Service agents are GS-1811-designated federal employees with the official titles "criminal investigator" and "special agent," while Uniformed Division Officers are federal police officers. Today's Secret Service Uniformed Division came about when the Secret

Service absorbed the White House Police Force and their responsibilities.

In contrast to the special agent's primary responsibility, which is to protect the physical body elected to the U.S. presidency, the Uniformed Division's primary role in the presidential security plan is to protect the White House structure, whether the president is physically present, or not. Notice the difference here, because this is where the media frequently screws up the reporting of security incidents at the White House. The agents secure the physical body, not the White House structure. Therefore, if a fence jumper at the White House jumps the fence when the president is not at the White House, then there is a slim chance that special agents will intervene to stop it, because they would be with the president on the road, not at the White House. But you'll frequently hear media figures report that the fence jumpers where apprehended by "agents," when in the overwhelming majority of incidents, they were not apprehended by agents, but by Uniformed Division officers. It may seem like nit-picking, but this persistent mistake drives many agents crazy because, as we saw with both Omar J. Gonzalez (the north-grounds fence jumper who made it all the way into the White House in late 2014) and Jonathan Tran (the north-side Treasury Building fence jumper who made it all the way to the south portico of the White House), it was primarily Uniformed Division personnel, not special agents, who were responsible for the security lapses. I am not pointing this out to pile on the Uniformed Division. After all, the special agent side has had their own share of debacles, ranging from the Colombia scandal to the two agents caught taking selfies with President Trump's grandson. I am pointing it out because diagnosing and fixing the security lapses at the White House requires that we identify the correct set of personnel, or else there's little chance of fixing the problem. Also, it hurts morale on both the agent and the Uniformed Division sides of the Secret Service when one side, having little responsibility for a security problem, is held to account for something they didn't do. I, along with a number of other still active agent friends of mine, have vivid memories of the Omar Gonzalez fence-jumping incident and the widespread Secret Service mockery that followed. Although I had long since resigned from the Secret Service, I remember being at my daughter's bus stop, waiting for the bus to pick her up, when a few of my neighbors were laughing at the incompetence of the Secret Service "agents" because they couldn't stop a war veteran with a bad knee from leaping the north-lawn fence and making it into the White House. They were surprised when I informed them that the agents had left just minutes earlier with President Obama from the opposite side of the White House as he departed for Camp David on Marine One and that it was Uniformed Division personnel involved in the breach. Ironically, it was an *off-duty* special agent from the Counter Assault Team who tackled Gonzalez on the State Floor of the White House and stopped a disturbing incident from becoming a disastrous one.

The Gonzalez fence-jumping incident was a catastrophic security failure on the Uniformed Division side, yet the failure was inevitable given the treatment of, and the poor management of, the rank-and-file officers of the Uniformed Division. I spent nearly five years as a Secret Service agent assigned to the White House as a member of the PPD, and I cannot recall a time where the Uniformed Division officers were treated with the dignity and respect afforded to police officers in the streets, where I worked as an NYPD police officer. Thankfully, most people will have limited interaction with police officers throughout their lives. It's this limited interaction that maintains the air of mystery surrounding police work and, I believe, provides for the high degree of respect most people have for police officers. It's rare to find an adult who doesn't remember playing "cops and robbers" while growing up, and few people would dispute the fact that it takes a tremendous amount of bravery to be a police officer. So, why is Uniformed Division police officer morale consistently poor as measured by job satisfaction surveys and anecdotal reports? I attribute some of the mistreatment of the Uniformed Division officers, and the corresponding morale problems, to the familiarity many of the employees at the White House have with the Uniformed Division officers. Unlike the average American citizen, who rarely interacts with police officers, the White House personnel see the same Uniformed Division officers every day when reporting to work at the White House complex. And as a result of the familiarity, many of the officers have subsequently been treated as second-rate security guards when working because the allure and mystery of the police officer brand wore off. Nearly every Uniformed Division officer I spoke with at the White House when I was assigned to the Presidential Protective Division had a troubling story about a member of the White House staff who had mistreated them. This mistreatment would often happen at the magnetometer checkpoints at the White House staff entrances. The dreaded "Do you know who I am?" line was a common component of these horror stories. Ironically, the Uniformed Division officers who would tell me these stories said that it was rarely, if ever, senior White House staff members who would engage in this type of obnoxious behavior with the officers. One officer told me that the degree of the obnoxious, and pretentious, behavior was inversely cor-related with the degree of access the White House staff member had to the president. During the George W. Bush years, complaints about the pretentious behavior of senior advisers such as Karl Rove or Fran Townsend (both had reputations for treating both Uniformed Division officers and special agents with respect and dignity) were unheard-of, but it was quite common to hear complaints about low-level staffers, and new White House employees, treating the Uniformed Division officers like a bunch of servants. Compounding this problem was the oft-reported complaint that the sergeants and the lieutenants of the Uniformed Division wouldn't back up their officers when a staff/officer conflict happened. Officers would relay to me that they were told to "just let it go," even when they were unquestionably on the right side of the dispute with a White House staff member. This may seem like a minor complaint, but low morale due to mistreatment by Uniformed Division management and some members of the White House staff was extremely destructive to the security posture of the White House because of the officer attrition that resulted.

The persistently low Uniformed Division officer morale, combined with the mediocre pay compared to other federal law enforcement positions, created a witch's brew of conditions for a death spiral of attrition to set in among the Uniformed Division officer class. The officers of the Uniformed Division, due to their necessary proximity to the president, are granted a difficult-to-obtain top-secret security clearance as a condition of their continued employment as officers. Once this security clearance is granted to the officer, it becomes a tradable commodity in the constantly churning Washington, DC, law enforcement/intelligence community job soup. It wasn't uncommon for me to be working a midnight shift at the White House, and chatting with a rookie Uniformed Division officer, only to find out the next night that he had left to take a position somewhere else, either within the federal law enforcement or intelligence community, or within the government consulting field where a top-secret security clearance is a game changer on a résumé. This caused severe problems within the ranks of the Uniformed Division because as more officers resigned, the ones who stayed behind were forced into double shifts and unmanageable work schedules, which further destroyed morale for the officers left behind (sadly, the same phenomenon that occurred on the agent side of the Secret Service). As this attrition death spiral continued over the course of years, the Uniformed Division was left with an experience vacuum for mid-career officers. The veteran officers, close to retirement, typically remained with the Secret Service, despite the poor working conditions. They had already invested nearly two decades of their lives with the Uniformed Division, and they weren't going to forfeit that experience to start over somewhere else. But the newer officers turned over at unmanageable rates as they became more experienced, obtained their security clearances, and built up their résumés. This left the Uniformed Division stacked with inexperienced rookies, afraid to make waves at the White House because the management was likely going to abandon them, and officers close to retirement who were in FIGMO mode, as it was called (F--- It, I Got My Orders)—in other words, "I'm outta here soon, so leave me alone."

Given the poor management, the even worse treatment by the White House staff, and the attrition problems with the officers of the Secret Service Uniformed Division, it's no surprise to observers of the Secret Service, active and retired alike, that both Omar J. Gonzalez and Jonathan Tran were able to circumvent the White House security plan, the sensors, the Emergency Response Team (also members of the Uniformed Division), and the officers on duty during both of these infamous incidents.

There are some solutions to the Uniformed Division problems that the Secret Service should strongly consider. First, although I strongly support limited government spending, the Secret Service will continue to struggle to retain officers in the Uniformed Division if they do not pay them commensurate with the inflated cost of living in the Washington, DC, metro area, where most of their officers are stationed. This is simply a function of basic arithmetic. Suppose Uniformed Division Officer Smith makes X amount of money as a Uniformed Division officer at the White House but has to put up with rude staffers, terrible hours, and a Uniformed Division management that throws him "under the bus." Then Officer Smith is offered a job at a Washington, DC-based consulting firm requiring the top-secret security clearance that he already has, and for more money than the officer is making with the Uniformed Division. Of *course* Officer Smith is going to leave. The Uniformed Division pay scale must be fixed to reflect the competitive DC job market for security-cleared personnel or the attrition death spiral among their officers will continue.

Second, the special agent side of the Secret Service should be assigned internship-type training days where they are assigned to learn about, monitor, and eventually oversee the Uniformed Division's White House operations. The special agents assigned to the White House work alongside the Uniformed Division officers whenever the president is physically present on the White House grounds, yet each side knows little about what the other side does. This knowledge gap creates a corresponding lack of understanding between special agents and officers, along with a noticeable friction between the officers and the agents. This damages morale on both sides. I knew many of the Uniformed Division officers by last name only, and unfortunately, when I was assigned to the White House, I couldn't tell you much about their shift rotations, their work hours, or their specific roles during a "crash" (Secret Service jargon for a White House intrusion). The special agents spend so much time drilling and rehearsing their specific roles in an intrusion, and potential evacuation of the president during a crash, while focusing intently on physically moving the president, that they are largely blind to the security of the White House structure, many figuring "Uniformed Division's got that." But if the agents assigned to the White House were nearly as familiar with the White House structural security plan as they were with the evacuation plan, then I'm sure the Jonathan Tran intrusion in March 2017 wouldn't have happened as it did.

Tran jumped the north fence of the Treasury Building and then jumped two subsequent fences on the southeast side of the White House to access the south grounds. Unbelievably, Tran nearly made it into the White House while President Trump was physically present. The location of the incident is critical because the external east side of the White House, where Tran made his way to the south grounds, is an area where the president rarely goes (he stays mostly contained to the East Wing residence and the West Wing), and for that reason most special agents aren't as familiar with that White House territory. The alarms in this area, and the zones, are all numbered, and I'm reasonably confident that many of the agents working that night both in the Secret Service operations center, and with President Trump at the White House, were unsure of the exact location of the crash and the intruder. Focusing more on officer and special agent cooperation through "internships" would do wonders to solve the information gaps among the agents and officers. It would also help build camaraderie between a Uniformed Division that sees itself as the redheaded stepchildren of the White House, and the special agents of the Secret Service, who would benefit greatly from an expanded base of knowledge about the structural security plan at the White House.

Third, the Uniformed Division must engage in a vigorous hiring effort to both replenish and stabilize its workforce. An increase in officer manpower would allow them to dramatically increase their personnel presence at the White House. A critical problem I often noticed at the White House was static posting with limited "pushes." A "push" in the Secret Service is a break, and asking Uniformed Division officers assigned to late-night and overnight shifts to stand in the same spot for hours at a time while maintaining maximum alertness and response capabilities is absurd and defies human physiology. Movement, and fresh eyes, are key components of any security plan, and expecting an officer to stand and stare at a door in the White House, with just a few breaks over an eight-hour shift, is problematic. Fatigue, distraction, boredom, and even counting exercises (I'm not kidding; an officer once told me that he would keep his mind occupied by counting the components of the ornate crown molding on the White House State floor) are just a few factors that can render an officer assigned to the White House less-than-effective during a crash. If the Uniformed Division doubled the officer personnel at the White House, then the officers would be constantly moving around to "push" each other. And with each moving officer, a fresh set of eyes, not one that has been staring at walls for hours at a time, would be set upon the White House terrain. Fresh eyes notice things that tired eyes often miss, and this can be the difference between a security success and a mission-critical failure. A heavy rotation of officer manpower also provides for backup personnel during a White House crash, and it would cure some of the crushing morale resulting from long shifts staring at the White House walls, which haven't changed in decades.

Fourth, an increase in officer personnel would also allow the Uniformed Division officers to train to appropriately defend the White House. Can you fathom asking a football team to execute a successful series of plays that they have rarely practiced? In sports, the movements and the coordination between the players on the field must be rehearsed repeatedly to overcome the tendency to overthink a response, rather than react. A credible White House crash with an active intruder is a serious and stressful event. Stress causes inescapable biological responses, including dilated pupils, accelerated breathing, and the loss of fine motor skills. The only way to overcome the debilitating effects of human biology, and defeat these stress-caused physiological responses, is to repeatedly train under simulated stress conditions. The repeated drilling of a defined motor response can assist a law enforcement officer in overriding the natural biological response to stress and to more efficiently respond to a threat.

In 2014 an independent panel, known as the United States Secret Service Protective Mission Panel, formed in response to multiple Secret Service organizational failures. Shockingly, a December 2014 report submitted to Congress by the panel exposed the shameful fact that for fiscal year 2013 "the Uniformed Division *as a whole* received 576 hours of training, or about 25 minutes for each of over 1300 Uniformed Division officers."[1] Twenty-Five minutes of training per officer? Think about that. If you work on an advanced assembly line, or at a consulting firm, there's a darn good chance that you received more job training in a month than the officers assigned to protect the most targeted facility on earth, the White House, received in a year. There's an enormous chasm between talking about a response to a White House crash, and actually walking through the physical motions of the crash response in a training exercise. I have little doubt that the clear lack of training, and the lack of urgency to reinstitute a rigorous training program, contributed to the Uniformed Division mess—and has left the president of the United States vulnerable to attack in the White House.

3

THE EVOLVING THREATS FROM THE "BIG SIX"

IT WAS MARCH 2007, and I was staring out of a slightly smog-stained window on the upper floor of a Bogotá hotel, at the picturesque Colombian mountains. There was a hint of fog on the mountains, which blended in seamlessly with the green trees, and the vista served as a welcome distraction from the nonstop stress of the upcoming presidential visit by President George W. Bush. I had been a special agent with the Secret Service for eight years at the time, but I was still relatively new to the Presidential Protective Division, and this was my first major protection assignment with the PPD. A senior agent who served as a mentor to me once described being a Secret Service agent as "the longest job interview in the world." He was right. Although Secret Service agents go through a nearly yearlong training program at both the Federal Law Enforcement Training Center in Brunswick, Georgia, and the Secret Service Training Academy in Prince George's County, Maryland (known as the JJRTC, or the James J. Rowley Training Center), nothing can prepare you for the stress and persistent anxiety that accompanies you while attempting to design a security plan to thwart the numerous potential attacks against the president. The senior agent referred to the evolution of a Secret Service agent's career as "the longest job interview in the world" because every noteworthy assignment an agent was given served to "check a box" (another expression used frequently among agents) on a long checklist of security assignments that was largely informal, but understood by special agents as a barometer for a successful Secret Service career.

I was approximately halfway through the career "checklist" when I was assigned to secure the Colombian presidential palace, the Casa de Nariño, for President Bush's 2007 visit to Bogotá, Colombia. The presidential palace had been attacked using mortars and projectiles just five years earlier, injuring three soldiers, and the looming threat of another attack while President Bush was present was causing me a lot of lost sleep during the protective advance phase of the Secret Service security operation. Compounding the anxiety was my poor health at the time. I had returned to the United States from Panama prematurely just weeks earlier due to illness, and I still wasn't feeling well. I had contracted dengue fever while on a protection operation in Panama City, Panama, with First Daughter Jenna Bush, and when my fever spiked to over 103 degrees, the Secret Service supervisor overseeing the operation made the decision to send me home to recover. Knowing that there was a fixed and limited period of time while assigned to the Presidential Protective Division to "check the boxes," I didn't take much time off to recover. When I arrived home, I asked the operations section of the PPD to plug me in if they had an open assignment for a "major site" security assignment.

A major site security advance was a necessary box to check to be taken seriously as an agent on the PPD. The checklist progression works like this: New agents to the PPD are first assigned to secure airports because most U.S. and international airports have been advanced many times before. Also, most major airports expecting a visit from Air Force One already have detailed security plans in place, which the Secret Service supplements with their own personnel and equipment. After successfully securing an airport, PPD agents are assigned a small, non-airport site to secure. An example of a small site would be a "grip and grin"–type of event, where the president goes to a home or office building and shakes hands with a limited number of people, typically followed by a short speech. These small sites are challenging for new agents to the PPD, but the small crowds, limited floor space to secure, and easy-to-manage flow of people and press make them ideal opportunities for newer PPD agents to learn the critical skills necessary to secure the life of the president.

Upon successful completion of a small site security plan, a PPD agent is then given a major site security advance "box" to check. If a sitting president has a limited travel schedule (as many 1980s-era special agents experienced with President Reagan, who had a limited foreign and domestic travel schedule after the assassination attempt at the Washington, DC, Hilton), then these major sites can be difficult assignments to acquire because of their scarcity. And if an agent doesn't successfully complete a security plan for a major site, then the "box checking" stops, along with his or her career advancement on the PPD.

Knowing the potential scarcity of major site security assignments got me back on my feet quickly despite still recovering from a severe battle with dengue fever, a battle that cost me twenty-plus pounds of body weight and sapped me of nearly all of my energy. Even getting dressed was a struggle while recovering, but when a friend of mine in the PPD operations section called me on my Secret Service–assigned BlackBerry and said there was an opportunity approaching for a major site advance in Bogotá, if I was up to it, I jumped at the opportunity.

After hanging up the phone, I immediately dragged my still-hurting body (the well-deserved nickname for dengue fever is "break-bone fever") out of bed, put on a suit, and drove into the White House complex to collect the materials and information for the major site in Bogotá. I was going to check this box even if it caused lasting damage to my body.

One of the WHMO (White House Medical Office) doctors had warned me in a phone call a few days earlier, while checking up on me, not to return to South America until I was completely recovered because the human immune system can work against you once you contract dengue fever. If you acquire a different type of the infection a second time, you can contract hemorrhagic fever, where your organs bleed internally and death is a possibility. Although the idea of liquefied organs scared the hell out of me, I knew if I didn't take the assignment, then someone else would jump on it. I was all in.

And that's how I wound up on the upper floor of the hotel room in Bogotá, staring at the beautiful mountain views. I was staring out the window, and not working on my security plan for the presidential palace, because I was patiently waiting to speak with the lead advance agent on the trip, "Nick." Lead advance agents on foreign security advances were the most respected advance agents in the Secret Service. Only the best of the best agents were permitted to act as lead advance agents overseeing the security of the life of the most powerful man on earth while in a potentially dangerous foreign country. After competing with hundreds of agents for the extremely limited spots on the PPD (only a handful of spots open up each year, and most Secret Service agents will never be selected to protect the president full-time as a member of the PPD), then you have to compete throughout your career on the hypercompetitive PPD with fellow agents to check the boxes and advance your career. After conducting a successful major site advance, then an agent would be in line for a logistics assignment. Logistics advances are a nightmare. Logistics agents are responsible for getting every agent, vehicle, weapon, and piece of security equipment into a foreign country and making sure everything arrives both on time and in working order. There is no room for error for a logistics advance agent. You cannot forget a presidential limo at home in the United States or leave it behind at a foreign airport because a customs official in a foreign country is being difficult. You can't forget to assign a flight or a hotel room to a PPD shift agent assigned to guard the president's six (a military and law enforcement term for providing rear coverage) and then tell that agent to stay home. It doesn't work that way. This is why a logistics advance assignment is the final box to be checked before being assigned to lead advance school, where PPD agents learn the skills necessary to act as a lead advance agent.

Logistic assignments separate the wheat from the chaff, and if a PPD agent can keep it together and manage international logistics successfully, then that agent can move up into the rarified air of lead advance agents. That's where "Nick" found himself on the Secret Service PPD career ladder during the Bogotá, Colombia, trip. Nick wasn't only the lead advance qualified agent on the PPD Bogotá advance, but he was one of few agents on the PPD who had checked enough boxes to qualify as a foreign lead advance agent. Acting as a lead advance agent within the United States was a difficult assignment because domestic lead advance agents are responsible for everything that happens on the presidential visit. Although the airport agent, the small site agents, the major site agent (me during this Colombia trip), the transportation agent, and the logistics agent all work for the lead advance agent on a presidential visit, the top supervisor on the PPD, the SAIC (special agent in charge) will deal almost exclusively with the lead advance agent on a presidential visit. That means that even if I were to blow it at the Colombian presidential palace by designing a terrible security plan, "Nick" would also be the one to feel the wrath of the SAIC.

I respected Nick, as did most of the agents on the PPD, and I was waiting to speak to him in that hotel room because I needed some guidance on handling the overwhelming number of name checks the Colombian intelligence services had given me. While talking about how to conduct the name checks, we veered off into a larger discussion about how to handle and prioritize threats to the president. That's where the "big six" conversation started. Nick told me to spend the majority of my time developing plans to neutralize threats from tactical assaults, medical emergencies, chemical/biological agents, explosives, airborne assaults, and fires. Although it was a simple way to sum up the threat picture, it served as a guide for me for the remainder of my career. Threats from the big six will haunt you throughout your career as a Secret Service agent as you develop new and creative ways to learn to react to threats as quickly as the terrorists and assassins can create them. Making matters worse is the evolving social media ecosystem and twenty-four-hour news cycle. The omnipresence of cell phone cameras and social media platforms has made every American with a social media presence, and a cell phone, a potential celebrity reporter. This has made this generation of political candidates and politicians extra-sensitive about their public personae, which just decades ago were only "public" if you saw them on the news, on the streets outside the Capitol, or at a county fair. Now, every breath, utterance, and action has the potential to end a politician's career because a camera or recording device is rarely more than arm's length away. No sound bite will be left spared if some entrepreneurial citizen or reporter can get it recorded.

This possibility of being recorded at all times has made the extremely stressful job of being a Secret Service agent almost impossible. For example, put yourself in the shoes of the Secret Service supervisor on duty with Hillary Clinton on September 11, 2016. As the world watched the solemn remembrance of the September 11, 2001, attacks at Ground Zero, many noticed Hillary Clinton exit the event suspiciously early. Despite some initial spin, Fox News Channel's Rick Leventhal accurately reported that Mrs. Clinton left the event early due to a "medical episode."[1] And a now-infamous video taken by a private citizen would later show Mrs. Clinton struggling to stand on her feet, and nearly collapsing, as a Secret Service van pulled up to the curb and escorted her from the scene. I was an instructor in the Secret Service academy, and I was a program manager for the rewriting of the Secret Service investigative training course for new agents. I know what agents are taught in the Secret Service training academy because I helped write and teach the curriculum. I took part in hundreds of mock emergency medicine and AOP exercises (assault on principle drills where we rehearse the response to a mock attack), and I cannot recall a single episode where an actor playing the president, or another Secret Service protectee, in a training exercise pretended to lose consciousness and the response was anything other than to immediately seek out a hospital or advanced medical care. But that's not what happened on September 11, 2016, with Hillary Clinton and her protective detail. She was taken to her daughter, Chelsea's, apartment in Manhattan instead. And although I obviously was not in the apartment with Mrs. Clinton at the time, I can definitively state that the medical care she likely received there was not qualitatively similar to the care at New York City's finest emergency rooms. Now, to be clear, I am not trying to pin blame on the Secret Service agents on Mrs. Clinton's detail on that day. The purpose of this book is to highlight some of the pressures facing the Secret Service, the necessary fixes the Secret Service must make to avoid succumbing to these pressures, and what will inevitably happen if the Secret Service doesn't evolve and change the way it currently conducts the business of protection. The country cannot, and should not, accept a Secret Service where emergency medicine and critical security decisions during potentially life or death moments are unduly influenced by political decision-makers.

4

THE THREAT OF A TACTICAL ASSAULT ON THE PRESIDENT

IT WASN'T A COINCIDENCE THAT NICK, the lead advance agent from the Colombia trip, named the tactical assault first when discussing threats from the big six. The grave threat to the life of the president of the United States from a trained team of well-armed, body armor–clad terrorists is difficult to manage, even for the elite agents of the PPD. The threat is so serious that the Secret Service protection model relies heavily on law enforcement and military assets outside of the agency to help counter the threat from a tactical assault. While coordinating security for a portion of the inauguration route on Pennsylvania Avenue for Barack Obama's first presidential inauguration in 2008, a prominent member of the broadcast media asked me, "How do you guys do all this?" I responded, "*We* don't." I wasn't suggesting that the Secret Service wasn't responsible for the security of the president. I was trying to emphasize to the media figure that though we, the Secret Service, design the security plan, it's a largely symbiotic effort between the Secret Service, the military, local police, and state and federal law enforcement that enables the Secret Service to manage enormous security undertakings such as a presidential inauguration.

If the Secret Service were forced to protect the president with no help from outside agencies and law enforcement personnel, the president would undoubtedly be put in immediate and grave danger. The Secret Service doesn't have the manpower or local expertise to secure every street corner the president visits during his time in office. Moreover, the Secret Service cannot during a weeklong security advance (the average length of a difficult security advance), match the lifetime of accumulated local intelligence in the minds of the dedicated local law enforcement, many of whom have spent years patrolling America's streets. The Secret Service, with few exceptions, has always maintained a strong working relationship with local and state law enforcement because they have to. Unlike the FBI, and other federal law enforcement agencies, where the relationship can be tense at times with local law enforcement, as jurisdictional fights, and the ever-present fights for access to classified information, muddy up the jurisdictional waters, the Secret Service cannot perform its basic and most important job, keeping the president safe, without outside help.

Imagine security around the president as a series of concentric rings, with access to each ring determined by the level of training, and the specific job function, of the agent or officer. The outer and middle security rings are almost exclusively the domain of local and state law enforcement personnel under the watch of a smaller number of Secret Service agents. There is a sensible reason for this concentric ring structure, and the use of local law enforcement personnel to man the middle and outer rings. No one knows the neighborhood terrain features, the local "players," and what should and shouldn't be in a neighborhood, like the local police officers. Years of patrol experience have trained the eyes of our nation's local police officers to spot anything out of the ordinary,[1] and any terrorist assault team using explosives and automatic rifles to initiate a tactical assault will most likely begin their assault on the outer ring first. They begin here, far from the president, because the ring of magnetometers surrounding locations the president visits have been pushed out farther and farther as the threat from suicide vests, and other explosives, has grown. It does the Secret Service no good to place their magnetometers just feet away from a location the president may walk by because a bomber could approach the magnetometer checkpoint and detonate before walking through. The trained eyes and ears of the nation's local law enforcement officers are the front lines of protection against the nightmare tactical assault that would stress even the most well-designed Secret Service security plan. Having them on the outside perimeter is a significant force multiplier that can stop an attack in a parking lot, rather than on the inside of a secure venue.

The stress and chaos of having to deal with multiple attackers, loud explosions, blinding and deafening percussion blasts, and rifle rounds whizzing past Secret Service agents and law enforcement personnel at thousands of feet per second, is tough to replicate in a training environment. I remember being a young agent-in-training at the Secret Service training facility in Maryland and going through a "Hogan's Alley"–type exercise where agent-trainees walk down the street and then all hell breaks loose. Instructors, in the role of the OPFOR (opposition force), pile out of buildings and start firing at the trainees, and the agent-trainees are expected to respond using their tactical training. To add pain to the training scenario (pain is a terrific training tool for training young agents what NOT to do), the instructors used Simunition rounds in their training weapons. Simunition rounds are plastic bullets with a soapy-textured, colored substance in the plastic round to mark where the Simunition round lands when it hits a trainee. It happened to be a very cool late-autumn day that training day, and we always hated Simunition training on cold days. The plastic rounds hardened up significantly in the cold weather, and if they hit you in the hands during the training exercise, then you would be in serious pain for the rest of the day, and you would have trouble moving your fingers. Aggravating the situation was that many tactical shooting exercises like this would naturally result in hits to the hands because the one thing both sides, the OPFOR and the trainees, are always focused on during the back-and-forth shooting is the opponent's gun. And the gun is always in the hands.

During this particular exercise it was my turn, and I began my slow stroll down the street, with its many false storefronts for instructors to hide in and pop out of. About three-quarters of the way down the street, I began to wonder if the instructors had forgotten about me (something that I mistakenly did as an instructor when the roles were reversed years later), as nothing happened. But no such luck. As multiple attackers in dark-blue, Secret Service–issued battle dress uniforms appeared in the street, I immediately sought cover. The OPFOR had waited to attack because as I walked farther and farther down the street, all of the quality cover to hide behind had disappeared (*cover* is the tactical term for a relatively bullet-resistant object that you can hide behind for protection, such as a car, or a wall). Concealment is another option that may or may not provide bullet-resistant cover, but does conceal you from the line of sight of the OPFOR (for example, a thin piece of pipe and drape). The only cover available was a small fire hydrant, but when training in a Simunition gunfight scenario, you take whatever cover you can get to avoid being pelted with endless Simunition rounds. I was approximately 185 pounds at the time and I'm six feet tall, but after being pelted by about four or five rock-hard Simunition rounds, in all of the wrong places (yes, use your imagination), I squeezed my body behind that small fire hydrant and fired back. I even hit a few of the OPFOR instructors and managed to get them to move back before the exercise ended. This kind of repeated tactical training, where there is a real penalty for using poor tactics (being struck by a painful Simunition round), is the only effective way to train the agent-trainees of the Secret Service to respond to the inevitable tactical assault that awaits them in the future.

Try to imagine a continuum of stress in a Secret Service emergency where a "level three" stress scenario is a lone gunman, with a handgun, caught hundreds of yards away from the president before he fires his weapon. Then imagine a "level ten" stress scenario on the stress continuum being a fifty-man assault team, firing high-powered automatic rifles, with body armor–penetrating rounds, and men and women being brutally mowed down all around you as you struggle to gather your senses in order to locate and evacuate the president. The training scenario where I sought cover behind the small fire hydrant was a one or two on that stress continuum. But even at that low level of training-induced stress, you quickly learn to respect what level ten would feel like. During the scenario, I vividly remember imagining how horrible the situation would have been if the Simunition rounds that were striking me in the arms and legs, and other painful places, were real bullets, not training rounds. This is the kind of mind-set you must train yourself to live with if you expect to succeed in the Secret Service. You must put aside the dread of being on the business end of a terrorist's rifle and put the life of the president first, and all of your fears a distant second. And although that fear is subordinated in favor of action after a long period of tactical training, it never really disappears. That fear serves as a motivational tool that agents use to work long into the night, on very little sleep, to avoid staring at that business end of a terrorist's rifle in a tactical assault that some terrorist group, somewhere in the world, is planning right now.

But does the management of both the Secret Service and the Department of Homeland Security have the collective will to battle political pressure and to modify the tactics and the training of the Secret Service in order to respond to the nightmare tactical assault that is undoubtedly coming? I know many of the working agents and first-line supervisors in the Secret Service, and many of them are asking the same question. First, let's analyze why the threat of a tactical assault on the president is growing and evolving.

Terror groups, such as ISIS, al-Qaeda, and their affiliates, have embraced suicide as a strategic weapon, and this dramatically complicates security planning for the Secret Service. Before the rapid growth of suicide attacks using small arms and explosives, the Secret Service would allocate security assets to areas where cover and concealment were available, and a viable escape route was available to the attacker. If an agent is securing a motorcade route for the president that's close to ten miles long, it's virtually impossible to secure every square foot of the anticipated motorcade route; therefore, when planning the assignment of local police officers and Secret Service agents along the route, a good agent assigns those assets to the most likely place from which a threat would originate. Before the use of suicide attacks (which obviously require no escape route), as a standard terrorist strategy, an agent could reasonably assume that forested areas, abandoned buildings with back doors, adjoining highways, and elevated platforms would be the most likely places from which an attack would initiate. An attacker would have the benefits of concealment, possibly cover, and a means to escape during the chaos in those types of environments. But the evolution of the terror threat has thrown that playbook into the garbage can. A growing number of these radicalized terrorists have no interest in cover or concealment; they're only interested in body counts and carnage. These killers have no need for a highway or access road escape route because many of them aren't looking to escape; they're looking to kill, and kill themselves in the process. If you watch the videos from the *Charlie Hebdo* terror attacks in Paris, you will see a clear example of this. The terrorists weren't hiding behind garbage Dumpsters, seeking cover. They were spending most of their time exposed in the street, screaming terrorist propaganda, and they were in no rush to escape. And for an extended period of time, they didn't even appear to be looking to leave the scene of their attack. Their priorities were media attention, propaganda dissemination, and accumulating as large a body count as possible. Escape and evasion appeared to be an afterthought.

The evolving threat of a tactical assault on the president that could originate almost anywhere, not simply from locations with an escape route, and with cover and concealment, will make future presidential visits to locations anywhere outside of the White House grounds difficult to secure with today's technology and protection models. There simply aren't enough police officers and Secret Service agents to secure every building and forested area on a motorcade route. But there is a way to begin to counter this evolving threat: quality pre-protection-operation intelligence. The Secret Service maintains a number of field offices around the United States, and around the world, even though the likelihood of a presidential visit to many of the small cities and remote towns these field offices cover is close to zero. The Secret Service maintains these field offices to conduct criminal investigations in their respective jurisdictions, but also to build and maintain critical working relationships with local law enforcement agencies. It is these local law enforcement agencies that are often the source of the most usable pre-attack intelligence, and they will likely remain so in the future as terrorists continue to attempt to infiltrate refugee populations from terror-ravaged countries. Refugee populations subsequently spread throughout the United States' less densely populated cities and towns. (Note: the Secret Service doesn't produce intelligence because of its sensitive role and proximity to the world's leaders, but it does consume intelligence related to its protectees.) But rather than law enforcement at the local and federal levels narrowing down and perfecting the art of intelligence gathering in communities where the threats to the United States, and the president, are originating, many of these agencies are retreating due to political pressure. Many law enforcement agencies, such as the NYPD, are under intense pressure from both national and local political leaders to avoid surveillance of places where practitioners of Islam congregate. These artificial, and unnecessary, limitations constrain our law enforcement officials from doing their jobs. Imagine a scenario where an NYPD organized crime detective assigned to the Russian organized crime squad is forbidden to surveil locations where Russians congregate. Does this sound ridiculous? That's because it is ridiculous, and it's dangerous. The Russian mob would quickly figure out that they are operating in a law enforcement vacuum and adjust their meetings and tactics to ensure that they plan their illicit activities in locations where law enforcement is forbidden to go. (Note: just as surveillance of the Russian mob in no way implicates all Russians in organized crime, surveillance of suspect locations of radical Islamic activity in no way implicates all practitioners of the faith in the activities of a few radical terrorists.)

I wish I could tell you otherwise, but a tactical assault on the president is likely being planned right now. Terrorists seeking media attention for their heinous acts have long understood that a successful attack on the president of the United States is the ultimate prize. Either harming or killing the president provides terrorists with universal media attention, which assists them in establishing credibility among terror financiers and new recruits, but it also gives them an opportunity to directly strike at the political head of our government, causing chaos through the resulting national psychological trauma. And the growing use of suicide tactics as a component of the assault greatly expands the attack options of the terror strike team because there isn't a need for cover or concealment, or the need for a viable escape route. The only way to react to a threat such as this is not to just react, but to be proactive via quality intelligence gathering and analysis, which will allow law enforcement and the Secret Service to intercept a planned tactical assault on the president before it happens. But even this necessary component of protection planning is being stifled by political pressure to provide extra justification for investigations involving threats from Islamic-inspired terror groups. Many of my law enforcement sources have told me that investigative leads are being left on the table and not properly investigated because of the pressure to provide unimpeachable, documented reasons for opening up terror investigations within Islamic communities. The fear of being labeled an "Islamophobe" by interest groups committed to using our legal system and public pressure to encourage law enforcement to look the other way, keeps many potential terror investigations locked in a desk drawer. We've already seen the tragic outcomes of these "known-wolf" terror attacks with Orlando night club terrorist Omar Mateen, Fort Hood terrorist Nidal Hasan, New York and New Jersey bomber Ahmad Rahami and, the most disturbing case of all, Anwar al-Awlaki. Awlaki was a vocal al-Qaeda cleric and terrorist recruiter who was interviewed multiple times by the FBI after the September 11, 2001 attacks.[2] The FBI and the NYPD cannot break up a terror cell from a case trapped in a dusty file cabinet. And the Secret Service will never be able to proactively stop the presidential assassination it never hears about due to political pressure suffocating investigations before they can begin.

Politics is impacting the Secret Service protective mission in other ways not immediately obvious to even the experienced observer. I spent most of my first year as a Secret Service agent providing protective advance work for Hillary Clinton during her U.S. Senate campaign. I was working in the Melville, Long Island, office of the Secret Service at the time, and the office had a limited staff of agents. The small staff, combined with the frequent trips by Mrs. Clinton to both Nassau and Suffolk counties (the areas covered by the Melville office) in Long Island, put me in frequent contact with Mrs. Clinton, her staff, and her PPD Secret Service agents. It was clear from the start of her U.S. Senate campaign that our lives in the Melville office were going to be made miserable by this campaign. As I stated earlier, one of the primary responsibilities of the Secret Service agents in the field is to maintain a strong working relationship with the local law enforcement officials for both investigative and protection purposes. The Secret Service relies heavily on these local law enforcement officials for both physical protection manpower on the outer and middle rings of protection, and for the critical intelligence that largely local law enforcement has the contacts to develop in order to disrupt any potential attack on the president. Maintaining good relationships with local law enforcement was exceedingly difficult when dealing with the Hillary Clinton for U.S. Senate campaign because Mrs. Clinton's staff would constantly complain about the visible presence of the local police at the sites she visited. I obviously couldn't read Hillary's mind at the time, but in my conversations with her staff, it appeared that they wanted the uniformed police officers hidden and tucked away, to give Hillary the appearance of approachability. "Approachability" was the same reason given for the use of what we called the "Scooby Doo" van. Mrs. Clinton shunned the use of the standard First Lady limousine package and used a ghastly-looking brown van for transportation instead, thinking that it made her appear more approachable. The political decision to keep the local police officers at a distance, and the decision to use the "Scooby Doo" van, was a nightmare for the Secret Service agents in the Melville office. First, the use of a stock van built for family travel, not tactical efficiency, caused enormous headaches for the Secret Service armorers, who had to ensure that the vehicle met certain standards for bullet resistance. Additionally, the van was extremely difficult to operate in any tactical driving scenario because of its height and weight. If the van was fired at from multiple angles, it would be a challenge to rapidly speed off and navigate turns at high speeds. In short, the Secret Service management team should have shut the decision to use the van down early and negotiated a better solution, but politics and "approachability" got in the way. Second, the local police in Nassau and Suffolk counties, understandably, didn't take kindly to constantly being told to "back off" by the Clinton campaign staff. It became a recurring hassle trying to soothe hurt Clinton staff members' feelings whenever they would see a small cadre of uniformed police officers securing a road intersection near a site Hillary Clinton was scheduled to visit. Can you blame the local police management for being upset? They were hardworking career men and women who had spent their working lives policing their respective areas and creating both safety and security. No police officer or police manager wants to be known for letting an area descend into criminal chaos, for both moral and professional reasons. But, it didn't appear that the Clinton Senate campaign cared about any of this. If they saw uniformed police officers in areas they didn't approve of, and they thought the "optics" were bad and that it made Mrs. Clinton look unapproachable, they would raise the issue with the Secret Service supervisor responsible for her protective shift, who would then bring the issue to my boss in the Melville office. Rather than focusing on securing the life of Mrs. Clinton, this charade caused us all to waste inordinate amounts of time politely requesting that uniformed police officers move slightly to the left, or slightly to the right, so that Mrs. Clinton couldn't see them. This back-and-forth dance with the police officers at these protected sites was a disgrace. The Secret Service works with local law enforcement to create a safe and secure scene for both the protectee and the people attending the protectee's event. Asking local police departments to hide themselves like misbehaving children, in the corner of a classroom, was humiliating for agents like me, who were police officers before joining the Secret Service. And more important, it was humiliating to the hardworking cops just doing their jobs and helping the Secret Service accomplish the mission. With the growth of phone camera and video technology, I expect this trend to grow worse in the future as Secret Service protectees, the president included, demand improved protection "optics" and they empower their inexperienced staff members to insert themselves into, and change the security plans, depending on how "approachable" they look. Never forget: terrorists planning a group tactical assault with heavy weapons and explosives are looking for "approachable" protectees too.

Defending against an organized tactical assault on the president is an extraordinarily challenging task and is one of the Secret Service's essential protective responsibilities. How can the Secret Service be expected to design security plans to defeat a small team of terrorists, with heavy weapons and explosives, when the rings of security, which are heavily reliant on the support and manpower provided by local law enforcement, are compromised due to political concerns, not security concerns? The Secret Service managers I worked with understood the need to balance the accessibility needs of Secret Service protectees against the security needs of the protectee, but Secret Service upper management must resist the urge in the future to roll over under pressure from protectees and their staffs to dramatically alter security plans because they don't meet some hard-to-define political aspiration of "approachability."

I suspect some Secret Service managers went along with these ridiculous security requests because they wanted to be liked by Mrs. Clinton, and they wanted to avoid any career-damaging controversy (which the Clintons would have unquestionably caused for any member of the Secret Service standing in their way). The natural instinct to be liked by the protectee is a tough one to suppress. I fell victim to it at times while assigned to Jenna Bush's detail. Jenna was always very friendly and easy to work with, but conflicts would inevitably develop, and it was tough to do the right thing, and not the easy thing, when you know the right thing is going to cause a fight with your protectee. Being around Mrs. Clinton constantly as a result of her travel schedule and campaigning probably caused some of the same conflicts with the Secret Service managers on her detail. I know many of the members of Hillary's PPD detail knew that the local cops were growing tired of the "run and hide" routine, but they would ask our Melville office team to make the request to move the police officers anyway. Mrs. Clinton had no issue airing her displeasure with things she didn't like, and I'm sure the PPD agents assigned to her wanted to avoid being lectured by her in the "Scooby van" after an unapproved police "sighting." Also, a call from Mrs. Clinton to Secret Service headquarters would be very damaging to any Secret Service agent's career if that agent were the subject of that call. Mrs. Clinton's security arrangements, because of this recurrent conflict with the local police, became more of a lesson in conflict avoidance rather than physical security. It's a miracle nothing happened to her because of this, but due to the evolving threat of a tactical assault from committed terror groups, there are no guarantees in the future if protection becomes about the optics of "approachability" rather than sound protection tactics. Local law enforcement, in uniform or not, are a Secret Service agent's best friend, and they are their first line of defense against the ever-present threat of a tactical assault. Secret Service management, in the future, is going to have to resist the urge to allow protectees such as Hillary Clinton the opportunity to treat them as political pawns to be shuffled around as they see fit, while compromising both their safety and that of the Secret Service.

The evolving threat of a tactical assault is compounded by the threat presented by evolving weapons technology. The detection of weapons is a mainstay of Secret Service security planning, and the use of advanced, nonmetallic materials for weapons construction may render much of their current technology useless in the future. Three-dimensional printing technology, and the evolution of advanced polymers will make it possible in the near future to construct deadly weapons in the comfort of your own home or business, and this technology has the potential to render the government regulation of firearms nearly impotent. In the future polymer-based firearms, built using a home-based, 3-D printer, will be easy to construct and will be limited only by access to the software codes necessary to build these weapons. The Secret Service relies heavily on the use of magnetometers to detect weapons, but this dated technology relies on the presence of metal to function. Although technology currently exists, and is in use in many of our airports, that uses body scanning rather than metal detection, the Secret Service is going to have to overcome its tendency toward bureaucratic inertia to move toward an agency-wide overhaul of its current magnetometer-centric security planning. Better weapons detection through advance screening mechanisms using technology that already exists, a rededication to cooperative intelligence sharing with both federal and local law enforcement partners, a strong Secret Service management culture that fights back against protectees who politicize security, and the continued evolution of the Secret Service training program to ensure its agents are regularly exposed to the stresses of simulated combat in a tactical assault, are all steps the Secret Service can take today to ensure the threat of a catastrophic tactical assault on the president remains just that, a threat, and not a reality.

5

THE THREAT OF A PRESIDENTIAL MEDICAL EMERGENCY

HAVING AN ARSENAL OF FIREARMS and impact weapons capable of handling everything from an unusual interest case (that guy who refuses to let go of the president's hand while shaking it on a rope line) to a terrorist hit team with belt-fed automatic weapons, is critical to both discouraging and countering an attack on the president. But it's only a small piece of the presidential protection puzzle. We live in the real world, and in that real world the everyday threats the Secret Service encounters are more likely to come from a medical emergency involving the president than they are from a tactical assault by terrorists. I was both a student and an instructor at the Secret Service training academy, and a significant portion of the special agent training program is spent learning how to deal with a presidential medical crisis. The agents are trained to be skilled first responders because the advanced medical care, if necessary in a medical emergency, will be provided by military medical assets traveling with the president on every trip. The Secret Service's training program trains their agents to effectively, and under intense stress, stop bleeding from an open wound, stabilize a broken bone, stabilize the head and neck, deliver oxygen, and take other immediate emergency medical actions in the moments just after a medical crisis.

The Secret Service repeatedly drills their agents and trainees on easy-to-recall emergency response medical actions during their training programs because agents will likely use their emergency medical response training only in scenarios where the fight-or-flight physiological response has taken over. Place yourself in the shoes of a senior Secret Service agent standing in front of the presidential podium as the president is delivering a speech to thousands of people in an arena, and millions more on television. I've been there, and it's a surreal feeling that encourages temporary attention lapses as you notice the unusual behaviors and mesmerized stares of people seeing the president for the first time. As an agent on the presidential detail, you have to be hyper-attentive to your surroundings, and the condition of the president, at all times. There is no room for daydreaming on the PPD. But, when you're standing in front of the klieg lights with the leader of the free world, it's exceedingly difficult to maintain 100 percent focus. I was always fighting the urge to mentally wander off to what my daughter was doing at school or why that man in the third row of the speech location is wearing that awful lime-green sweater to a presidential speech. Secret Service agents are human beings too, and as their careers progress, they learn, as I did, to drown the noise out and to pay attention to the details that matter, such as inappropriate crowd behavior and hidden hands. But no amount of training can teach an agent to act like a robot. If the president were to collapse onstage during a speech, the Secret Service agents surrounding him would immediately respond, but there's little doubt that temporary chaos would ensue. Media figures would be trying to report the breaking news while their camera operators and photographers would be trying to get the best shot of the fallen president. The crowd would quickly grow concerned and would need to be controlled to avoid a stampede. The White House staff would respond to the stage, desperate to control the ensuing narrative and to protect the president's image. And all of this would create an environment of unimaginable physiological stress for the first Secret Service agent to arrive at the president's side. But that agent must control his emotions and act, because the moments immediately following a serious medical crisis can be the difference between life and premature death. In the critical early moments of a medical emergency, it is absolutely essential that certain steps be followed, and to ensure those steps are followed, the Secret Service trains their agents to "look, listen, and feel." This is familiar to any emergency responder, and it's a quick way to remember to look for the chest rising and falling, to listen for breathing at the mouth and nose, and to feel for a pulse. It is these easy-to-remember bullet points that enable agents under stress to easily recall their training without having to engage in higher-order mental gymnastics, which can be lost while responding to a medical emergency under stress. But there was another training tip I learned as an agent trainee in the Secret Service academy that I worry will never apply to the Secret Service again after the events surrounding Hillary Clinton on September 11, 2016: "check, call, and care."

There are few areas as uncontroversial in the security field as the appropriate response to a medical emergency, but the Clintons have a penchant for politicizing everything they touch, and the Secret Service response to a medical emergency may never be the same after Hillary Clinton's medical episode on September 11, 2016. During a memorial ceremony commemorating the victims of the September 11, 2001, terror attacks, which I described earlier in the book and which Mrs. Clinton attended, she left the event earlier than her scheduled departure. Mrs. Clinton's early departure elicited some attention from the media representatives on the scene because there had been some earlier media speculation about her fitness to be the president of the United

States based on scattered reports of poor health. As a video later showed, Mrs. Clinton appeared to lose consciousness temporarily as her Secret Service detail escorted her into an awaiting van. I was taught in Secret Service training that during a medical emergency involving the loss of consciousness of a protectee, we should "check, call, and care": check the scene for danger, call 911, and care for the protectee. These steps are modifiable, depending on the severity of the medical emergency, but after reviewing the tape of Hillary Clinton nearly collapsing while attempting to enter her Secret Service van on September 11, 2016, I'm convinced politics took precedence over her health during the incident. Unfortunately, the Clintons appear incapable of separating any decision they make, about their health or otherwise, from the resulting political ramifications. They have spent their entire lives in the political arena, and they have learned to consider each decision not on its moral, ethical, or health merits, but on the resulting political capital to be gained or lost by that decision. I have little doubt that the agents working on Hillary Clinton's detail on the day she nearly collapsed at the September 11 memorial ceremony wanted to take her to a hospital for evaluation. But in the heat of a contentious political campaign, where questions about her health continued to surface, the pressure from the campaign staff appeared to have won out. As stated in chapter 3, Hillary Clinton didn't go the hospital after her health episode that day. Instead she retreated to her daughter's apartment, where the campaign staff, and the political voices around her, could focus on handling the narrative they wanted to spin about her health, rather than ensuring that she wasn't in the midst of a severe health crisis. Thankfully, Hillary reappeared later in the day in front of an eager outpost of media representatives, anxiously staged in front of her daughter's apartment, and appeared to be fine, but it didn't have to turn out that way. If her health had taken a turn for the worse, the agents assigned to her that day would have been ruthlessly second-guessed for their actions. And the political decision makers who may have had a role in her avoiding the hospital would have likely faded back into obscurity, avoiding any blame whatsoever. It's precisely these types of pressures in this new era of twenty-four-hour-a-day news coverage, ubiquitous cell phone cameras, and social media postings that the Secret Service is going to have to deal with in the future.

Secret Service management, as with the pushback they've received from the Clinton camp and others on the "optics" of uniformed police officers at Secret Service–secured sites, must be prepared for pushback in the future when a protectee medical crisis demands that they respond in a manner suited to save the life of the protectee, not to spin a media narrative. It's not the Secret Service's job to ensure that in the tragic event that the president faints and hits his head on the ground, the people surrounding him don't use their phones to take a video of the event. These videos may be embarrassing on the evening news, but the videos won't kill the president. The lack of medical attention in a medical crisis, due to political concerns over health concerns, will.

6

THE THREAT TO THE PRESIDENT FROM CHEMICAL/BIOLOGICAL ATTACKS AND EXPLOSIVES

ASSASSINATIONS, ASSASSINATION ATTEMPTS, AND WARFARE through poisoning, chemical, and biological attacks have been used primarily by states or state-sponsored actors. The 2017 assassination of Kim Jong-nam, the estranged half brother of North Korean dictator Kim Jong-un, using a nerve agent; the 1988 chemical gas attack on the Kurds by the Iraqi military, which killed thousands; and the 2013 and 2017 gas attacks on Syrian civilians by the Syrian Army are recent examples of state-sponsored chemical attacks. Another was the near-lethal poisoning of former Ukrainian president Viktor Yushchenko, which was likely carried out by state-sponsored actors. And although these tactics aren't completely foreign to terror syndicates and small group actors, as we saw with the 1995 sarin gas attack in the Japanese subway system by the group Aum Shinrikyo, and smaller chemical attacks in the Middle East by known terror groups, these types of attacks are exceedingly difficult to pull off without the backing of state actors. Despite the ready availability of preparatory information on the Internet, these deadly chemicals and biological agents are extremely challenging to prepare and store without eliciting the attention of law enforcement officials. Once prepared, many of these chemical and biological agents also require a delivery mechanism to disperse them among the intended victims.

A growing problem for the Secret Service with regard to the chemical/biological weapons threat is detection. The bureaucratic inertia of the Secret Service often prevents the agency from responding proactively to growing threats, but this threat is uniquely dangerous, and the agency must respond as such. Given the grave danger of this threat to the president, and to Secret Service protectees, I must be cautious in this chapter not to divulge any operational details that would put our agents at risk. With that caveat stated, the Secret Service does extensive planning to prevent losing a protectee to a chemical/biological attack. The Secret Service has a special team dedicated exclusively to the decontamination of the president and his immediate protective detail, but decontamination is far different from detection. The Secret Service should prioritize the training of their hazardous agent detection teams, and they should immediately recruit from the military and scientific communities the best chemical/biological weapons experts they can find and use them to train for attacks using these chemical/biological agents. It is only through the repetition, under stress, of a simulated attack training-stimulus that the Secret Service personnel assigned to the hazardous materials teams will uncover the holes in their detection, decontamination, and evacuation plan.

The use of chemical/biological weapons presents a number of additional complications for the Secret Service outside of the physiological complications from such an attack. For example, are there extra clothes around to cover the decontaminated personnel after the immediate attack? Clothes would be immediately stripped off, and as I discussed in the last chapter, the political figures surrounding the president would be understandably concerned about the "optics" of a seminude president being decontaminated or dragged from an attack site. Do not underestimate the power of political "optics" and the pressure constantly put on the Secret Service to do things that make their protectees look good, rather than taking actions that make them safe and secure. I'm concerned that in a questionable chemical/biological attack scenario (one where a suspicious powder is found on or near a protectee, but its status as a weapon isn't confirmed), the growing pressure on the Secret Service to engage in a political response rather than a decontamination response will be overwhelming—and potentially deadly. The hazardous agent teams in the Secret Service must be assured of the support of Secret Service management in the unfortunate event that they must take action in a questionable scenario such as the one I just described. Sadly, when I was an agent, I heard from agents often on the PPD and in the Uniformed Division at the White House who feared acting out of precaution and then being thrown under the bus by Secret Service managers. It's tragic that with a pressing threat such as the one from chemical/biological agents that the concern of many of the Secret Service personnel would be support by management, but it was very real when I was on the PPD.

The threat to the president from the tactical use of explosives is another evolving threat that keeps many Secret Service agents up at night. The recent wars in both Iraq and Afghanistan have been instructive for U.S. military personnel. They have learned how to respond to the evolving tactics of our enemies, but those wars have also been instructive for our enemies, who are learning to evolve to our technology as well. Our enemies are learning how to modify explosives into explosively formed penetrators (EFPs), which are shaped to penetrate the armored vehicles our military use in the war zone to transport personnel. Many of these EFP attacks have been lethal in the war zones, and they led to the military's development of newer transportation platforms, such as Mine-Resistant Ambush Protected (MRAP) vehicles with V-shaped bottom halves to disperse the blast pressure from improvised explosive devices, or IEDs. This is an area where the Secret Service has done a superb job. They are so concerned (appropriately so) about the threat from an EFP, or an improvised explosive device attack, on their armored vehicles that they are constantly working with both private industry and entities within the U.S. government and military to improve their vehicle armoring technology. The Secret Service has a full-time crew of personnel exclusively dedicated to winning the dangerous "explosives versus armor" technology race, and their approach to armor technology is evidence of the agency's ability to do things correctly when the management puts aside politics, and personal ambition, to fix a problem.

7

THE GROWING THREAT TO THE PRESIDENT FROM THE SKIES

WHEN I JOINED THE SECRET SERVICE IN 1999, the threat of a potential attack on the president from the skies was expected to originate from small planes and helicopters. After the September 11, 2001, attacks on the World Trade Center and the Pentagon, that threat analysis changed. Although Secret Service security advances had considered the threat of an airborne assault from the skies using a hijacked jetliner in the years before the September 11 attacks, the gravity of the threat became tragically transparent after the September 11 attacks occurred. Ironically, as the airborne threat evolves, the primary threat to the president has morphed from the passenger jets used in the September 11 attacks to small, miniature, and micro-sized drones.

Drones present a number of security complications for the Secret Service. A small, commercially available, modern drone can be used as a delivery mechanism to carry and drop an explosive device on the secure grounds of the White House, causing both damage and chaos (a method already being used by terrorist organizations against U.S. forces on foreign battlefields). Or, a micro-drone the size of an insect could be flown into the White House complex and used as a nearly undetectable surveillance tool. A miniature, unarmed drone can also be used to tie up limited Secret Service surveillance, uniformed officer, and agent assets while a secondary assault takes place elsewhere on the White House complex. The threat of distraction while a secondary assault takes place, taking advantage of the protection assets bogged down with the distraction, is nothing new to the Secret Service. But a distraction from the sky, using a drone, is a new type of threat.

When I was an instructor in the Secret Service training academy, we used a training scenario for protection exercises where trained role players and training staff would pretend to be members of a crowd on a presidential rope line. The role players would pretend to fight at one end of the rope line while a mock assassin would fire his training weapon at the person playing the role of the president from the other end of the rope line. New agent-trainees frequently got baited into the distraction and would miss the real threat from the assassin at the other end of the rope line. But seasoned agents returning to the training academy for in-service training rarely fell for this same stunt. Distractions from the sky, whether planes, or drones, create additional security complications for an obvious reason; Secret Service agents and officers cannot fly. Investigating a ground-based threat such as an alarm break on the White House grounds is usually as simple as an agent or Uniformed Division officer walking over to the area where the alarm was tripped and clearing it, or apprehending a suspect. The overwhelming majority of the time, these alarm notifications are wildlife walking across the White House grounds at night and are quickly cleared, creating a minor distraction for the White House protection personnel involved. But airborne alarms create a multitude of security headaches because they require some technological intervention to clear the alarm or take down the drone.

Drones have to be either physically removed from the secure skies over the White House by physically intercepting the drone, or by intercepting the drone's communications from the drone operator. The drone threat is further complicated by rapidly advancing drone technology, which allows the drone to be flown automatically, without guidance and communications from an operator (in this complicated case the Secret Service should monitor the ongoing development of a new class of military lasers that can overload the electronics of a flying drone, destroying its capability to stay airborne). Disrupting the communications of the drone can allow the security personnel at the White House to land the drone and investigate if it is weaponized, being used for surveillance, or just a nuisance. All of these interventions require time and technology, and they present the Secret Service with a number of complications if the drones infiltrate the secure White House airspace in swarms. As I stated in the introduction, I know many of you reading this may be wondering, "Why give the bad guys any ideas?" That's a fair question, but I can relay to you with certainty that the "ideas" have been floating around among groups with ill intent for a long time. I wrote this book precisely because I am genuinely concerned that some of the sclerotic Secret Service upper management, who are entrenched and who refuse to evolve with the evolving threat environment, will not acknowledge the seriousness of this threat and boldly respond to it. I'm also convinced that Secret Service management may avoid the necessary, major security overhauls that must happen at the White House until enough public pressure is put on them to respond. Many of the Secret Service managers making the critical decisions about the safety of the life of the president of the United States are career risk managers. They've learned to manage the risks to their own careers by not rocking the proverbial boat. Many of these upper-management personnel are just years from retirement and are looking at high six-figure postretirement jobs in the consulting or security services fields. They are not looking for a fight over a dramatic shift in the Secret Service security plan at the White House. They'll enact some token security measure to take a few drones down on the White House grounds, but they likely understand that the real threat comes from the more spectacular swarm attacks, and I'm concerned that they're doing little to defend against this very real threat.

Here's a real-life example of the managerial risk avoidance I referenced within the Secret Service. When I was assigned to the transportation section of the Presidential Protective Division located in Secret Service headquarters, I was asked by my direct supervisor to attend a meeting with a representative from a security company. The company had developed a secure satellite technology applicable toward monitoring the whereabouts of President Bush when he was riding his bike (GPS technology wasn't nearly as advanced at the time as it is currently). Although President Bush always rode with a peloton of staff, military, and Secret Service agents, he would at times veer far off course into the woods, and we would lose sight of him from the road when we were stationed in the motorcade. This was always a source of distress because if during those critical moments where we lost visual contact with the president from the cars, a Secret Service supervisor called out for his location on the radio, the agents in the cars wouldn't have a specific answer, and every agent listening to the back-and-forth radio traffic knew it. During the opening moments of the meeting, the representative from the security company began to describe what I felt was an elegant solution to this problem using his company's secure GPS technology. But not a few minutes into the presentation, the agent in charge of the division overseeing these types of acquisitions rudely interrupted him and shut down the meeting, saying the technology wouldn't work. I was embarrassed for him. The security representative had hauled his butt out to our headquarters, and he had a perfectly viable technology, solving a vexing security problem for the Secret Service, and he wasn't even allowed to finish his introduction before being shown the door.

This was not an isolated incident, as similar situations happened when I was assigned to the Secret Service training center operations section. I recall two companies that were looking to make their technology available to us, and also being preemptively shown the door. One company had a fire suppression chemical, which I thought was a good fit for the Secret Service advance teams working on overseas trips where the fire department was either nonexistent or ill prepared to handle a fire. The second product was a weapons system that allowed the operator to fire his weapon from around a corner, giving the operator a tremendous tactical advantage in a firefight. But neither of these products got a fair look because the company representatives never got past the e-mail and introduction stage. I saw this over and over again at the Secret Service, and it was events such as this that led the agents I worked with to mock the Secret Service's fear of new technology by saying the motto of the agency should be "The Secret Service; yesterday's technology, tomorrow." But as we saw with the proactive Secret Service effort to work with both the private sector and the military on armor technology for the Secret Service vehicle fleet, the management is capable of evolving with the current threats when they perceive the threat as either immediate enough or catastrophic enough.

Walk into many technology company corporate headquarters and you'll see pieces of their technological security puzzle, and their access-control mechanisms, putting the Secret Service's technology to shame. These companies have an incentive to control access to their facilities to avoid the theft of their technology, and many of them will spare no expense on retinal scanning, fingerprint access systems, and other modern access-control technologies. But the Secret Service operates differently. Many of their critical-decision makers in management fear the impact on their careers if they propose a solution for a spectacular attack, such as a drone swarm strike, because that attack is unlikely to happen on their watch. And they refuse to burn an ounce of their internal career capital (which many intend to use on promotions and on relationships with the private sector they plan to join in retirement) on changing a security plan that hasn't, in modern times, resulted in the loss of a president—yet.

But if the White House security plan doesn't evolve, and doesn't leverage technology to its advantage, then it will fail. It's solely a matter of when. The Secret Service must regularly consult with an outside consortium of technology leaders, military operators, and industry security leaders to consult on both its use of technology, and on an upgrade of the airborne security blanket surrounding the White House. They must develop and continuously improve an impenetrable "air defense" prepared to handle an infiltration of tens, or hundreds, of drones at a time. Mass interception of the drone's communications, along with physical interception of the drones, must be foolproof and immediate, and the detection technology for the drones must empower on-site Secret Service leadership at the White House to make immediate decisions on both interception and disruption. When an attack such as this happens, there isn't going to be time to make multiple phone calls to Secret Service headquarters staff, or to PPD management, to defeat the drones. The PPD special agents and Uniformed Division officers on duty at the White House have to be empowered to train with, be able to operate, and immediately use the anti-drone technology or they will be quickly overrun like a school yard by a swarm of wasps.

8

TRUMP AND TWITTER: A BLESSING AND A CURSE

THE TRUMP PRESIDENTIAL CAMPAIGN USED—and the Trump presidency continues to use—social media platforms such as Twitter in a manner never seen before in presidential politics. Although I've never run for the presidency, I have run for the United States Senate and the House of Representatives, and I'm familiar with the political consultant class and many of their robotic recommendations for candidates with regard to social media usage. Pre–Donald Trump, the generally accepted theory among the political consultants I spoke with regarding social media resembled the Hippocratic oath: "Do no harm." In other words, use your social media accounts to post innocuous, nonconfrontational political messages targeted toward a specific voter demographic and, critically, avoid unnecessary social media fights at all costs. Many of the political consultants and campaign managers I know do not even allow their political clients access to their own social media accounts out of fear that they may "do harm." The consultants insist on controlling the accounts as a preventative firewall in the event a candidate has an original thought and decides to post it to Twitter before focus-group testing the tweet. The Trump presidential campaign broke both of these "rules." Trump frequently fought with his political opponents on Twitter, and the more prominent the opponent, the more likely he was to get a spirited response. In addition, Trump's Twitter feed, although monitored by his campaign staff, clearly was his personal vehicle for many stream-of-consciousness tweets.

I have firsthand experience with Donald Trump and his creative use of Twitter because I was the subject of one of his tweets during the tail end of the 2016 presidential campaign. On August 9, 2016, I received a call from a booker at CNN asking me to appear that night on Don Lemon's nightly program. I was knee-deep in my own campaign for Congress in Florida's Nineteenth Congressional District at the time and was hesitant to agree to the appearance, but as is often the case with "gut feelings," something told me to do it. The booker, due to my Secret Service background, wanted me to comment on statements Donald Trump had made with regard to Second Amendment supporters and Hillary Clinton, which some in the cable news, talking-head class, had disingenuously portrayed as a threat to Hillary. The appearance quickly degenerated into a slugfest between me and the host, Don Lemon, as I defended Trump's comments, adding that in my professional opinion, this was nothing remotely resembling a threat. At one point, after being repeatedly talked over, I shouted at Lemon, "You don't know crap, Don!" I said this because it is true; he doesn't. Lemon was never a Secret Service agent, and he has zero experience in the threat-assessment arena. But I do. I was frustrated that he insisted on telling me how threat analysis worked, despite never having done it. This happens often with left-leaning media figures who outrageously assume that their faces on television anoint them with special insight into issues that actual experts don't have. I'm not sure if Donald Trump was watching my appearance on CNN at the time, but he either saw it or someone told him about it after the fact.

The next morning, a little after eleven o'clock, I glanced at the Twitter app on my mobile phone and noticed something odd: I had picked up a couple hundred new Twitter followers. Picking up a few hundred followers in a week was a social media milestone for me, so you can imagine my surprise to see a spike of a few hundred followers in just a few minutes. When I opened the app, I found out why the new burst of followers: Donald Trump had tweeted to me, thanking me for defending him on the CNN appearance. His tweet read, "@dbongino You were fantastic in defending both the Second Amendment and me last night on @CNN. Don Lemon is a lightweight—dumb as a rock."[1] I appreciated the gratitude, and by the end of the day, I had accumulated thousands of new Twitter followers. But not everyone appreciates the tweets of Donald Trump as I did. This is where the Secret Service enters the equation and must evolve to the changing social media environment.

The Secret Service has personnel assigned to their headquarters whose sole responsibility is to monitor and track presidential threats on the Internet and on social media platforms. When I joined the Secret Service in 1999, as e-mail was beginning to crowd out snail mail as the primary means of written communication, I remember conversing with protective intelligence agents and lamenting the fact that written presidential threats had just overcome a major obstacle: the stamp. The small obstacles of paying for a stamp and physically writing out a threat letter using a pen and paper were now eliminated, and anyone in front of a computer could e-mail a threat to the White House e-mail address. We all knew this was going to lead to an avalanche of new threats to be investigated. The explosive growth of social media platforms such as Facebook and Twitter eliminated yet another small obstacle to communicating a presidential threat: the need to search for a White House e-mail address. As I proposed in my 2013 book, *Life Inside the Bubble,*

I believe these factors were the primary drivers for the growth in the number of *reported* threat cases directed at President Barack Obama. Many in the media attempted to link the growth in threat cases to racism against President Obama, but I didn't notice any sudden surge in racism while I was on President Obama's personal protection detail. I did, however, notice an explosion in social media usage while Obama was the president, and with that increased social media usage came the ability to threaten the president of the United States by simply tweeting to him, or tagging him on Facebook, a process that requires little effort. And based on the absurdity of some of the threats I read as a Secret Service agent, it doesn't require serious intellectual capacity to type up an outrageous threat. This has caused the Secret Service innumerable headaches. They live in a zero-error environment where they cannot skip an investigation on a threat case, whether snail-mailed, e-mailed, tweeted, or Facebooked. But as a matter of simple logistics, they cannot possibly interview every person who takes advantage of social media to threaten the president.

Complicating matters for the Secret Service is President Trump's personal use of Twitter. While I cannot conclusively show that President Trump is the person physically tapping the keyboard and pressing Send for each tweet on his account, the evidence suggests that he personally monitors and uses the account (Dan Scavino Jr., President Trump's director of social media, confirmed this in an April 2017 interview with the Fox News Network[2]). There's a pattern to his recurrent tweets, evidenced by his use of punctuation, capitalization, and wording, that strongly suggests that he is the person sending many of the tweets. Unfortunately, this has fed the public perception that if he is the one sending the tweets, then someone wishing to threaten him can send him a tweet in response. This has led to an enormous number of threatening tweets directed both at Trump, using his Twitter handle, and in response to his own tweets.

The Secret Service does not have the manpower required to handle this volume of social media tweets. They will have to evolve with the changing "rules" for social media usage because Trump has reset the "rules" for what a president or presidential candidate can do on Twitter. How are political consultants going to reasonably tell their presidential candidates in future presidential campaigns that active, personal engagement on the platform is a strategic loser, given Trump's tremendous success doing precisely that? And since sending a Secret Service agent out in the field to investigate every Twitter threat (the volume of which is likely to explode in future campaigns) isn't a plausible option, the question is, what can they do? This will be uncomfortable for the Secret Service, but they are going to have to partner up with local law enforcement on PI cases. "PI" stands for protective intelligence (what I've been referring to as a threat case), and the Secret Service takes PI cases so seriously that every PI case is managed out of a headquarters division exclusively dedicated to PI case management. The management of the Secret Service has always feared turning over the management of PI cases to the field offices because the investigation of a presidential threat is an elaborate process within the Secret Service, and when a PI case is opened, it is difficult to close. Because of this elaborate administrative process, Secret Service headquarters was concerned that managers in Secret Service field offices would avoid opening PI cases to escape the massive mound of paperwork required to close these cases if they turn out to be false alarms. But this PI case investigation and management process was designed for an older era, when snail-mailed threats were relatively rare and phoned-in threats from landlines were easy to locate. In this new era of difficult-to-track e-mail and social media threats, the Secret Service is going to have to abandon this headquarters-centric approach to managing PI cases. They are going to have to turn control of these cases over to the Secret Service field offices, and the local Secret Service field offices will have to partner with local law enforcement to appropriately investigate these cases. The model for this isn't new. The Secret Service already does this with counterfeit currency cases. Counterfeiting U.S. currency, although limited in scope, isn't rare enough for the Secret Service to be able to run every case into the investigative ground. Therefore, to prosecute counterfeiters, the Secret Service works with local and state law enforcement on smaller counterfeiting cases to prosecute them through the local and state systems.

The Secret Service would be well suited to provide sophisticated training to local and state partners in order to move forward with a partnership on PI cases. There would likely be enormous managerial pushback from the Secret Service because of the fear of local law enforcement misdiagnosing a threat case (a potential attack that could have been prevented), but this is the only palatable choice they have. Unless the Secret Service plans on hiring tens of thousands of additional agents to investigate every late-night Twitter threat directed at the president, their choices are (1) pick and choose which threats to investigate or (2) decentralize the PI investigative model and train and trust local and state partners to help on PI cases.

9

TEMPORARY PROTECTION AGENTS, THE "WOW" FACTOR, AND WHITE HOUSE STAFF ASS-KISSING

THE SPECIAL AGENT MANPOWER CRISIS in the Secret Service has caused a cascade of problems throughout the agency. One of those problems became headline news in March 2017 when it was widely reported that two Secret Service agents, while transporting President Trump's eight-year-old grandson, Donald Trump III, snapped a selfie with him while he was sleeping in the back of a vehicle the agents were driving. Trump's grandson awoke in the middle of the photo, and his parents, Donald Trump Jr. and Vanessa Trump, were understandably disturbed by the incident. I was employed as an agent for over a decade, and I've taken many photos with protectees—some at their request, some as a courtesy to PPD agents, and some taken by members of the media—but I cannot fathom why two adults trained as Secret Service agents and charged with securing the life of an eight-year-old boy, would think it was appropriate to snap a selfie with a sleeping child. The creepy factor in this story is extraordinary, and when the story became public, a number of current agents I keep in contact with relayed to me that even the most forgiving agents were repulsed by the story. Most Secret Service agents are parents first, and many of them felt that this wasn't only an abdication of the agent's official duties; it was an embarrassment to the agency and the people working within it. But with the manpower crisis in the Secret Service, this event, however creepy, is explainable.

The Secret Service's two largest permanent protection details, the Presidential Protective Division (PPD) and the Vice Presidential Protective Division (VPPD), are difficult assignments for agents to get. Contrary to public perception, most of the Secret Service's special agents are not assigned to these protection details. Most Secret Service agent staff are assigned to investigative field offices. Due to their preference for experienced agents only, it takes a Secret Service agent anywhere from seven to ten years of above-average performance in his or her investigative field office assignment before that agent is eligible for reassignment to either the PPD or VPPD protection detail. This limits the pool of agents eligible for these assignments for a couple of reasons. First, not every agent assigned to a field office will be an above-average performer. "Above-average" would obviously be meaningless if there weren't an accompanying group of below-average performers in the field offices. Many of these below-average performing agents will be assigned to positions in intelligence, on the Dignitary Protective Division, or they will remain in the field office throughout their careers because no other division of the Secret Service will accept them. Second, the manpower crisis on both the Uniformed Division side of the Secret Service and on the special agent side has caused the Secret Service to hemorrhage mid-career officers and agents. This phenomenon is especially prevalent during the busy presidential election campaign seasons where younger agents, hired in the years immediately preceding a presidential campaign, and with no experience in dealing with the rigors of arduous workweeks on the campaign trail, leave the Secret Service relatively early in their young careers because of the shock of the campaign workload. (Note: the Secret Service has hidden some of their shocking attrition numbers in the past by classifying agents who leave for employment in other federal agencies as "transfers" rather than resignations.) As is the case with the Uniformed Division officers, many of the older, veteran special agents, have invested so much of their lives into the Secret Service that it becomes an indispensable part of their identity, and they stay with the agency, not wishing to start over later in life with another federal law enforcement agency. This leaves the Secret Service with a noticeable experience gap of mid-career agents, eligible to be assigned to the PPD and the VPPD, who are both still young enough to physically perform at an elite level in the protection mission, and experienced enough to avoid being prone to the "wow factor."

The "wow factor" in the Secret Service doesn't fit into a simple descriptive box, but most agents who have served any appreciable period of time in the Secret Service have experienced it. It's that feeling that younger, less-experienced agents get the first time they do _____ (fill in the blank) as an agent. I left the space blank because the Secret Service is so full of incredible experiences that I used to joke with people that it was the closest thing to being famous, without anyone knowing who you are. Most Secret Service agents have vivid memories of the first time the president of the United States walked by their post in the White House, or the first time they stood post outside of the Oval Office, or the first time they boarded either Air Force One or Marine One. Being a Secret Service agent is a job full of amazing firsts. I remember my first day assigned to the White House on the PPD as if it were just yesterday. I recall standing outside of the Oval Office on an afternoon shift for the first time and being overwhelmed by the fact that if, God forbid, something were to happen to President George W. Bush during the time I was assigned the Oval Office post, I was expected to act quickly, decisively, and without any hesitation to either save the president, or remove the threat. It really hits you like a blast of cold air after leaving a warm shower when you're first turned loose as a new agent on the PPD. The gravity of what you've been trained to do slams you in the face as you're posted in front of the Oval Office, and if you're as fascinated by politics as I was at the time, you can't process all of the information as people you've only come to know from their talking heads on the cable news channels walk by you and say hello.

I was impressed in my early days on the PPD how friendly everyone in the George W. Bush White House was to the Secret Service. It took a few months for the "Who's that guy? I know I've seen him on TV" internal questioning to wear off. Sometimes I would see a familiar face from Congress in the White House, and I would recognize the face but I couldn't recall the person's name. The irony was that many of the newer members of Congress who were at the White House for the first time appeared to have the same "Wow! I can't believe I'm here" look on their faces as some of the new agents to the PPD did. The "wow factor" is generally strongest while at the White House, as the awe the building, its history, and its prior occupants inspires is breathtaking. During my first overnight shift at the White House, I remember walking through the State Floor on the East Wing side and thinking about how many presidents and dignitaries had walked this exact path, and the dramatic domestic and global crises they must have been trying to mentally power through as they took each step on the echo-prone and cavernous State Floor.

Memories of my first trips on both Air Force One and Marine One also had a "wow factor." Although my first trip on Air Force One was a short one (less than an hour of flight time), I still remember walking up the back staircase of the plane and thinking that I was surely being mistaken for someone else. I couldn't fathom that I was doing what I was actually doing, even though I had been a special agent for nearly a decade at that point. I also remember the first time I flew aboard Marine One with President Obama. We were flying in the smaller UH-60 Black

Hawk version of Marine One, and the quarters were extremely cramped, but it was still a breathtaking moment. Flying in the helicopters in the Secret Service, whether aboard Marine One or on the support helicopters, is visually stunning because it looks like a motorcade in the sky. I remember flying by the Hollywood sign in Los Angeles as a passenger aboard one of "the birds" and thinking that I couldn't imagine doing anything else. It's as if the Secret Service agent position is two entirely different jobs. First, you're asked to be a cop, hunting down criminal counterfeiters and fraudsters, and then you're thrust into the world's most sensitive power centers with the most powerful people on the planet, and you're told not to be a cop but to be a diplomat, a security agent, and a psychologist. Despite what the Secret Service management continues to publicly state in order to hold on to the investigative mission (again, largely due to the potential for postretirement positions in the financial sector, which the Secret Service is charged with investigating as part of its financial crimes investigations), these two missions require entirely different skill sets with very little overlap. Some of the field agents who excel at criminal investigations go on to become below-average protection agents, and vice versa.

My initial experiences, and the accompanying emotions surrounding them, in the White House, aboard Air Force One, and aboard Marine One, are all examples of the "wow factor" (my sincere apologies for the ridiculous name, but there really is no sophisticated way to describe it). These experiences are emotionally overwhelming at first, even for the most experienced special agents newly assigned to the protection details, and it takes years to learn to treat the PPD as a job, rather than an experience. I know this may seem odd to the outside observer, because most people have only seen the Secret Service on television, and they are accustomed to seeing their stone faces devoid of emotion and hidden behind dark sunglasses. But this is a fantasy no different from a Hollywood movie filmed near the Hollywood sign I flew over aboard Marine One. Despite their stern, calm, and collected external demeanor, most of the agents on the PPD and VPPD, with the exception of a handful of senior agents who've been on the detail for years, are self-aware of the magnanimity of the task they are doing, and how special it is that they are doing it. Likewise, those agents are also aware of the penalties for screwing up the mission.

This is why the wow factor is so dangerous to the protection operations of the Secret Service. Every moment spent deliberating on how amazing what you're doing is, or how someone at home might see you on TV performing your job (note: I was not at all above this in my initial years on the PPD; therefore, I personally know the dangers of it), is a moment you may be distracted from observing a suspicious person in a crowd on a presidential rope line. Experience is a game-changer on the PPD, and it takes years on the PPD to learn how to drown out the external stimulation surrounding the president, and to focus exclusively on the protection task at hand. Yet, this is where the Secret Service has another glaring malignancy. The loss of many mid-career agents to other federal agencies due to the relocation requirement for agents, and the agent salary cap in the Secret Service, combined with the large size of President Trump's family, who all fall under the PPD protective umbrella, has created another manpower crisis within the PPD, with no end in sight. The agents assigned to protect the grandson of President Trump on that day in March 2017 were temporarily assigned to the detail from the field offices. They were not experienced members of the PPD. Even with newer and less-experienced agents assigned to the protective details, there's still an "I can't believe I'm here" component, and although the two temporarily assigned agents unquestionably should have known better, they were probably thinking about how exciting it was to be protecting members of the First Family. I am in no way apologizing for their behavior; I am simply trying to explain why two adult Secret Service agents would think it was a good idea to snap a selfie with a sleeping youngster.

I included the wow factor in this book about fixing the problems within the Secret Service not simply to discuss why a few agents took an inappropriate selfie, but also because this is at the core of a dangerous training deficit within the Secret Service. Being a new member of the PPD or the VPPD is an intimidating experience when agents first arrive, and learning how to speak up when you see something going wrong is a learned skill. It can be intimidating when an agent first arrives on the detail to tell a senior member of the president's advisory team, or a member of Congress, that he or she cannot enter the president's "holding room" (a room designated for the president where he can relax before or after a speech or event). The Secret Service is aware of the problem, and as a result, they assign new agents to the PPD to the "press agent" role for the presidential security shift because that's the position with the least amount of responsibility (the press agent has to ensure that the press stays "clean," meaning free of weapons and explosives after the security sweeps). And candidly, it's also the position farthest away from the president on a protective movement, where a less-experienced PPD agent can do the least amount of damage if he or she "shits the bed" (agent jargon for panicking when something goes wrong). But spending multiple shifts as the press agent is not enough training to wear down the wow factor to a degree that a PPD agent can function, agnostic of his high-octane surroundings. The PPD and the VPPD are currently so dramatically undermanned that fully staffed protection mission training has become a rarity. The White House is a ghost town during presidential domestic and foreign travel, and it's a travesty that during these times, the Secret Service isn't using the facility for intense protection training. It may surprise you to learn that in the nearly five years I was assigned to the White House as a PPD agent, I didn't tactically train on the White House facility even once. Even worse, in that nearly five-year period, I never once saw the inside of the residence on the East Wing side of the White House. Think about that. I was a "number one whip" on the PPD (a non-supervisory position but one that places you in charge of the president's protection shift while you're working at the White House), and I never saw the inside of the residence I was expected to respond to if there was an emergency involving the president. I had only seen maps of what the inside of the White House residence looked like. Talk about a wow factor. Can you fathom having to wake the president at night during a dangerous intrusion into the White House as the working whip and having to look at a map of the presidential residence to find your way around, while seeing the president and First Lady's sleeping quarters for the first time? To do this seamlessly, and without hesitation, these maneuvers should be drilled repeatedly, over and over, until the movements become instincts. This is the Secret Service; it isn't bouncing at the local bar. Every decision an agent makes in the Secret Service in a real emergency is going to be scrutinized in perpetuity, and every agent on the PPD knows it. If you make a mistake as a bar bouncer breaking up a fight in your bar and, it turns out, it's really just two friends messing around, it's no big deal, and the world doesn't really care. But if you're a Secret Service agent who has never seen the inside of the White House residence, and you're in charge of evacuating the president when multiple armed terrorists, with explosives and heavy weapons, start jumping the White House fence, and you turn left instead of right in the residence because the president got up to use the bathroom, then you just changed the entire course of world history. Local bars and bartenders don't have a wow factor, and the penalties for the bouncer screwing up in the circumstances I described are painless. But being a Secret Service agent means being surrounded constantly by high-octane emotion, majesty, and history that can be a powerful emotional distraction and can paralyze even the most-seasoned agent with thoughts of the devastating consequences of taking the wrong action in an emergency. This can only be overcome with consistent, rigorous, on-site training of very specific responses to emergencies, which can override the emotions of the moment of attack and allow the agents to effectively operate and maneuver in the physiological "red zone."

You may be curious why Secret Service management hasn't prioritized the training necessary to drill into their PPD agents the proper emergency responses at the White House. There are a couple of factors at play here. First, the manpower crisis within the Secret Service has rippled throughout the PPD and VPPD, and the constant search for personnel has forced them to assign temporary agents to the PPD, as was the case in the infamous Donald Trump III selfie debacle. This has severely curtailed the time allotted for training among the agents permanently assigned to the PPD and the VPPD. In a perfect world, PPD agents work two weeks of morning shifts, two weeks of evening shifts, two weeks of midnight shifts, and two weeks of training. But this perfect world rarely materializes because the management of the Secret Service, due to workforce constraints, doesn't prioritize the two weeks of assigned training. Agents on their two-week training rotation are routinely taken off of training assignments to conduct both "in-towns" (presidential security advances in the Washington, DC, area), and out-of-town advances, and the training is rarely made up. Compounding the training deficit is that the best advance agents are typically in high demand because of their ability to handle difficult situations on security advances. Therefore, these agents are routinely taken off of training to do advance work, and as a result, many of the best agents, ironically, rarely train. At the tail end of my PPD career, I was assigned to a number of lead advances, and as an advance advisor (coaching a first-time lead advance) so often that I found it difficult to find the time to perform even basic training such as my mandatory monthly shooting requirement with my service pistol. I gave up trying to do it during work or training hours due to the never-ending travel, and I started shooting during those increasingly rare off days. This infuriated my wife, but it kept me out of the PPD supervisor's office.

Even when PPD agents are permitted to train, the training rarely happens on-site at the White House. This is inexcusable and is largely due to the fact that the Secret Service management in headquarters is risk-averse and does everything in its power to avoid conflict that might damage their promotional potential or post-retirement work plans. Fighting for training time on the White House complex would ruffle some White House staff feathers because it would alter their work schedules, and it would alter the White House tour schedule for their friends and families. But it's absurd that Secret Service headquarters isn't making a strong push for it.

It's not entirely surprising that this fight for White House access isn't happening. The culture of the PPD imbues its agents with an unnecessary and dangerous sense of submissiveness to the White House staff, which carries over as the working agents become head-quarters managers themselves. The Secret Service could push the issue with the White House staff to allow it to conduct regular exercises within the White House, but that would disrupt the White House social calendar. When you've learned to do everything in your power to avoid conflict with the White House staff and be subservient, these are fights few Secret Service managers are willing to initiate, even though the lack of on-site training is one of the reasons behind the recent security failures at the White House.

I expect none of this will change until the Secret Service cleans house at the headquarters level and the DHS brings in outside eyes to see the training shortcomings currently staring the Secret Service in the face. Or, heaven forbid, a trained terrorist team of White House assailants successfully breaches the White House and has to be removed by a military special weapons team. I suspect that in the congressional testimony in the aftermath of such a devastating attack, it will be revealed that many of the agents on duty that day were never even offered the opportunity to train on the actual White House grounds they pledged their lives to defend.

Subservience to the White House staff was a hallmark of the Secret Service's PPD while I was on the detail. The obsequious behavior of the PPD management is not a natural trait inherent in most of the working agents on the PPD. Rather, it's drilled into them by a Secret Service management class primarily concerned with conflict avoidance, not in always doing what's in the best interests of presidential security. It was strange working on the PPD because, on the smaller issues that would pop up on security advances, I was always backed up by PPD manage-ment when the White House staff and I had conflicting views on how a presidential security plan should be implemented. But on the larger issues, such as the visibility of the Secret Service special weapons team CAT (the Counter Assault Team, which is the Secret Service's version of a SWAT operation), and the distance between the Secret Service agents and the president (the White House staff was constantly asking us to stand farther away from the president than we were comfortable doing in order to keep the cameras from picking up the agents—again, to make the president appear more "approachable"), the Secret Service would consistently lose the fight. The world saw the results of the White House staff's "keep the agents away from the president" cries during the infamous shoe-throwing incident during President George W. Bush's December 2008 trip to Iraq. I was working in the Washington, DC–based PPD Joint Operations Center (JOC) when the incident happened, and as the team at the JOC watched it unbelievably unfold on the many television monitors inside the old, dank, and cramped Joint Operations Center, we were in disbelief. Of course, the phones started ringing off the hooks in the JOC in the immediate aftermath of the incident, with Secret Service upper management looking for answers as to what happened. But we only knew what they knew from watching the television, because it had just happened. The working PPD supervisor that day was one of the finest men I ever worked with in the Secret Service. He was a noble man with a warrior's heart. I know that when he looks back on that incident, he wishes he'd been closer to the president than he was. But it wasn't his fault. The White house staff were obsessed with getting Secret Service agents "out of the shot," that is, away from the view of the TV cameras. Think about the insanity of this position. President Bush was in one of the most dangerous countries in the world for an American president to be in, Iraq, and the staff still wanted agents out of view. I'm hoping someone close to our current president reads about this silliness and asks the president himself to squash this potentially deadly, "stay out of the shot" nonsense before someone else gets hurt or embarrassed. Sadly, many of the PPD agents doing advance work knew that the management wouldn't back them up in a pissing match with the staff about these larger issues, so most of these fights were over before they started, because agents just refused to fight them.

This constant battering by the White House staff in the back-and-forth battle between presidential security demands and presidential "approachability" optics had a powerful psychological effect on the agents of the PPD when I was there, as they learned to succumb to an informal hierarchy in the White House where the PPD agents, unfortunately, are near the bottom. After years on the PPD, some of the agents learn to fight back and win many of these approachability-versus-security fights, but most of them do not. Also, many of the winners are unfairly labeled "troublemakers." This tone is set early in a PPD agent's tenure on the detail, and it is always set by the staff. With such a heavy responsibility for setting the tone for how the presidential "bubble" (the White House staff, the White House Military Office, the White House Communications Agency, and the Secret Service) should conduct itself and represent the White House when the president is traveling, a reasonable person would expect that the White House staff would act as an example for the other members of the "bubble," the Secret Service included.

When I left Barack Obama's presidential detail in December 2010, it was a poorly kept secret that people within his closest of inner circles had not only failed to set the proper tone for the behavior of the personnel within the presidential bubble, but had acted inappropriately on a number of foreign trips themselves. The behavior that the White House staff were engaging in during the Obama administration could have easily jeopardized our national security by putting sensitive information in the hands of suspicious foreign actors who may have been targeting these Obama staff insiders. But rather than stopping this behavior by confronting the protectee, or the White House staff, members of the "bubble" accommodated it, and Secret Service management ignored it, to avoid conflict with the staff, as if these people are earthly gods to be worshipped and never questioned. The election of Donald Trump was a loud message to the Washington, DC, elites that the American people were tired of this two-tiered system, but the power of the "bubble" is strong, and it reinforces this double standard of behavior.

Many of the Secret Service lead advance agents on overseas presidential trips quietly knew to have a late-night access plan ready in case these Obama administration staff insiders returned back to the presidential hotel late in the night, and in the early morning, with people unfamiliar to the advance team. I've never spoken publicly of this before, but I, along with a number of PPD agents I worked with, found it deeply troubling that many of the same Obama administration staff insiders who knew about the worst behavioral offenders within the Obama inner circle and spent time with them overseas, were quick to attack the nascent Donald Trump administration in its early days for suspicious ties to the Russian government, with little evidence backing up those claims. These former Obama insiders exhibited the worst kind of hypocrisy on Twitter, calling out the Trump administration, and putting them under an artificial cloud of suspicion, when many of these Obama acolytes knew about the recklessness and carelessness that happened overseas when their friends were occupying the White House.

I suspect many of the PPD agents who served during this same time period know exactly what I'm referring to regarding the reckless overseas behavior of many of President Obama's closest staff members, and many of them were bothered by it at the time. After the fence-jumping incidents and the Secret Service scandal in Colombia, it's public knowledge that the Secret Service has had its own share of problems overseas, and I'm in no way suggesting that the special agents of the Secret Service are free from sin, me included. Human beings make human mistakes, and the agents and officers involved in the fence-jumping incidents and the overseas scandals were punished severely (two of the officers involved in the 2017 fence-jumping incident were fired by the Secret Service not long after the incident) for their mistakes, along with being publicly, and privately, humiliated within the Secret Service. Their careers and their lives were never the same after their mistakes.

But what happened to the Obama insiders who engaged in equally troubling behavior? Nothing happened to them. Their reckless behavior, the kind that would have cost lower-level White House staff members their positions, was ignored. They continue to be the "go-to" talking heads for the former Obama administration, hell-bent on destroying the current Trump administration, and they're taking the country down in the process.

The Secret Service fears confrontation with the White House staff and handles complicated staff and Secret Service conflicts through the PPD management and White House operations chains-of-command. But if the White House chief of staff, or the president, were to instruct his team to be more accommodating, and less confrontational, with the Secret Service, and to include them as workplace equals during advance work, and not subservient security guards, the rank-and-file agents would likely be more comfortable coming forward and disclosing breaches of conduct that they've seen on foreign trips. Many of the Secret Service agents I remain in contact with have told me that the Trump administration has been taking steps to work with the Secret Service and to improve the information flow and working relationship between the members of the presidential bubble. It is comforting to hear that President Trump's operations staff within the White House has begun to open up to a more prominent advisory role for the Secret Service. Maybe then, with this new and more cooperative model, the Secret Service can begin to bury the troubled past with prior White House staffs and move forward with a less obsequious posture. This would ease the "wow factor" when working as a PPD agent in the White House and would encourage more responsible decision making, not subservient behavior designed solely to avoid conflict with Secret Service protectees and irresponsible White House staff members.

10

THE BROKEN WHITE HOUSE
SECURITY PLAN

THE EIGHTEEN-ACRE WHITE HOUSE COMPLEX is a dual security threat. Both the physical building located at 1600 Pennsylvania Avenue, and the president of the United States, who both works and resides inside the building, are top-tier targets for terrorists, hostile state actors, and psychologically disturbed individuals. Few buildings in the United States have been attacked as often as the White House. It has been attacked from the sky (during the 1994 Cessna crash on the South Lawn), from the north side (during the 1994 SKS rifle attack on the north grounds), and from the south side (during the 2011 sniper attack from Constitution Avenue). In addition, in just the past few years, two intruders,

Omar J. Gonzalez and Jonathan Tran, both mentioned earlier, made it onto the White House grounds on both the north and south sides, respectively. Gonzalez made it all the way to the State Floor of the East Wing of the White House before being stopped by an off-duty Secret Service agent. The White House is a magnet for attacks, and the main obstacle to appropriately securing the facility is that some of the White House stakeholders insist on treating the White House as a museum rather than as the most threatened government office building in the world. Making changes to the security plan at the White House is a complicated process because nearly every inch of the building is bound to a piece of history that someone is attached to and someone is convinced should be preserved. And while no one in the Secret Service I'm aware of is suggesting anything as dramatic as a complete redesign of the external grounds of the complex, they would likely meet heavy resistance if they were to put a substantive plan on the table to significantly modify the White House grounds to protect against today's threats.

The White House was designed to house the president in a far different security environment from the one we live in today. It wasn't uncommon when the White House first opened in the early 1800s for visitors to walk directly up to the front door of the building. And both East and West Executive Avenues were open to pedestrian foot traffic. Pennsylvania Avenue, on the north side of the White House grounds, was open to horse-and-buggy traffic, as was the area now encompassed by the fifty-two-acre White House Ellipse. But although there have been significant security upgrades at the White House since its construction, the upgrades are not enough to fix the security problems. The White House is in both a challenging location for security, Washington, DC, and within a challenging location within that challenging location, the business center of Washington, DC. The White House needs a dramatic security overhaul of its external perimeter to mitigate the growing threat of an organized tactical assault on the grounds, and thus far, Secret Service management has not been able to force these changes.

Here are some changes the Secret Service should immediately seek to implement at the White House to enhance its security footing:

1. The Secret Service should stop tinkering with the current White House fence. With the exception of the new "anti-climb" spikes added in 2015 to the top of the fence, the fence has not undergone any significant changes since 1965. The current White House fences on both the north and south sides of the White House will do little to stop an organized terrorist assault team from penetrating it and making way to the White House front and back doors. The White House fence was designed to stop people from walking on to the grounds, but it was never designed to withstand a blast from small yield explosives, or a strike from a vehicle, and both the Secret Service and the terrorists know this. The Secret Service made a small effort to combat the threat of an organized assault at the White House fence line in April 2017 when they announced that the south grounds fence line would be closed, and pedestrian foot traffic would only be allowed on the north side of the Ellipse. But this policy, although well-intentioned, will do little to stop an organized terrorist tactical assault team from assaulting the fence line. To prevent this, the Secret Service must start over and tear down the White House fence. It's a relic from a different era, littered with different threats, and it is an open invitation for people looking to do our president harm. In its place, the Secret Service should install an aesthetically pleasing double fence, wired with vibration sensors to detect movement, and angled outwards, which would make scaling the fence nearly impossible. The double fence should have enough distance between the two fences that Uniformed Division officers and K-9 teams can patrol the area and respond to threats rapidly. The fence should be high enough that, in conjunction with the angling outward of the fence, it should prevent scaling and the use of ladders to bypass it in an attack. And although no fence would withstand a blast from higher-yield, heavier explosives, the fence should be sturdy enough at its base to maintain some semblance of structural integrity in the event that a group of terrorists employs explosives in an attempt to breach it. Tearing down the current White House fence and replacing it with a

more technologically advanced fence with some of the specifications I mentioned will provide an enormous tactical advantage to the Secret Service when, not if, the White House is attacked by a committed team of heavily armed terrorists.

2. The Secret Service Uniformed Division should consider turning the Uniformed Division Foreign Missions Branch over to the State Department and immediately reassigning the Foreign Missions officers to the White House. The Secret Service's troubled history with mission creep has also impacted the Uniformed Division. The early 1970s expansion of the Uniformed Division's (then known as the White House Police) mission to include foreign diplomatic missions was a misguided one. The Secret Service provides unparalleled value to the American taxpayer in fulfilling its core mission, keeping the president of the United States safe and secure. And in a normal business environment, this would be known as a "core competency." But the Secret Service has always had a difficult time resisting the urge to expand its portfolio of responsibilities for reasons already discussed. Expanding the Uniformed Division mission to include securing foreign diplomatic missions does little to support the core mission of the Secret Service, which is keeping our president safe. The State Department has a budget far larger than that of the Secret Service, ranging from approximately $40 billion to $58 billion, depending on whether you factor in funds applied to overseas conflicts. The Secret Service's budget is approximately $2 billion, a fraction of what the State Department is allotted for overseas conflicts alone. The boldest way to solve this problem is to rid the government of the alphabet soup of federal law enforcement agencies, intelligence agencies, and inspectors general, and to combine assets from the different agencies into a larger, but more efficient, federal law enforcement operation where none of this jockeying for funds and responsibilities would be an issue. But I don't see this happening anytime soon. Lawmakers think small nowadays, and their interests are largely in reelection and parochial items. The boldness of our Founding Fathers has escaped

this generation of politicians, who prefer to remain on the ship while it's sinking rather than fix the leaks. In addition to the lack of political will to course correct the Secret Service among the political class, the Uniformed Division would likely resist giving up the responsibility for foreign diplomatic missions as well. Contrary to public perception, working at the White House is not a sought-after assignment within the Uniformed Division. Most officers would much rather be assigned to the Foreign Missions Branch of the Uniformed Division, where they can engage in patrol and actual police work. Uniformed Division officers assigned to the White House are largely relegated to fixed posts, which forces them to stare at walls and doors all day. After the allure of working at the White House wears off, which can happen after a few long, boring, days there, most of the officers want a break from the monotony. The Foreign Missions Branch has been that break because it allows the officers the freedom to police the areas around the foreign missions facilities and to do what's in their hearts, be cops. But the Secret Service simply does not have the manpower for this expanded role any longer. By dropping the Foreign Missions Branch responsibilities altogether, they could free up personnel for reassignment around the eighteen-acre White House complex, where many of the officers could be permitted to roam and patrol, and to break up the monotony of fixed White House posting. But there's another obstacle. The White House complex, and the surrounding streets, are a political hot potato when it comes to police jurisdiction. Governments are experts at creating unnecessary bureaucratic hurdles, and the White House policing plan is no different. As the plan currently stands, there are multiple federal and local police agencies that have their hands in the security plan surrounding the White House. This would prevent the Uniformed Division from reallocating Foreign Missions Branch officers to patrol roles in, and around, the White House. The Washington, DC, Metro Police Department, the U.S. Park Police, and the Secret Service Uniformed Division, share policing jurisdiction in the areas surrounding the White House, and these agencies would likely hesitate to give up their piece of the security pie. Whether an incident happens in the White House, on the sidewalk to the White House, on the streets surrounding the White House, or in the parks on both the north and south sides of the White House is determinate in deciding which of these law enforcement agencies has jurisdiction. Do you realize how absurd this is? Having a stew of law enforcement personnel, although dedicated and committed to their missions, surrounding the White House with different training, different weapons, different cultures, and different communications infrastructures, is outrageous and a lesson in government inefficiency. Here's an easy trade for lawmakers, and the Secret Service (which I have no illusions will happen because it's too simple, and the changes would hardly benefit any Congressman's reelection campaign): the Secret Service gives up foreign diplomatic missions security, and in turn, the jurisdiction for security of the White House, the surrounding streets, and the parks on the north and south sides of the complex are turned over to the Uniformed Division. This would finally give them the ability to do the police work around the complex that they crave, and have specific expertise in.

3. The Secret Service should expand the Emergency Response Team, the K-9 Team, and the Counter-Sniper Team presence at the White House. One of the bright spots for the Secret Service Uniformed Division is their special teams. Although the special agent workforce and the Uniformed Division officer workforce rarely interact outside of the White House and the vice president's residence, I've worked closely with many of their special teams members while doing advance work for Presidents Bush and Obama. Uniformed Division officers assigned to the K-9 and Counter-Sniper teams will routinely travel outside of Washington, DC, with the special agent advance teams from the PPD to assist in securing presidential sites both within the United States and overseas. I have always been impressed by the skill and work ethic of the members of the Uniformed Division special teams while conducting security advances. The K-9 unit dogs and the

Uniformed Division officers were always impressive in their ability to adjust to complex work environments (dogs don't adjust very well to time changes on long overseas security advances, and many of the K-9 team personnel had to learn to be diplomats in some majority-Muslim countries where dogs are not allowed in certain locations). Even on the most difficult of assignments (a visit to a foreign capital city, with multiple high-rise buildings, which is a sniper's paradise) the Counter-Sniper Team's work product was always timely, and appropriate to the threats. The Secret Service has some of the best countersnipers in the world. They routinely train to neutralize targets out to thousands of yards, and under difficult weather conditions. The Secret Service Counter-Sniper Team uses a JAR as their primary weapon. And in case you're thinking that JAR stands for something sophisticated, it stands for "just another rifle." Although the rifle is customized to fit the bodies of the technicians using them (officers assigned to the Counter-Sniper Team are called "technicians"), they are Winchester Magnum bolt-action rifles, not dramatically different from the commercially available version. In addition to the Counter-Sniper teams, the Secret Service deploys the Emergency Response Team (ERT) on the grounds of the White House. The ERT is the Uniformed Division's version of SWAT, and the officers assigned to the ERT must meet rigorous physical fitness and firearms proficiency requirements. The personnel assigned to ERT are some of the most skilled and tactically proficient officers the Uniformed Division has, and their footprint should be dramatically expanded on both the North and South Lawns of the White House. The physical and firearms capabilities of these elite operators are far superior to those of ideologically driven but generally poorly trained terrorist assault teams. And as for any concerns that an expansion of ERT Uniformed Division personnel would make the White House look like an "armed camp," this is nonsense. The White House north and, to a greater degree, south grounds have a multitude of places where ERT Uniformed Division personnel could patrol and dodge in and out of view of the public, which is always watching on the fence line. If the Secret Service ever combines an expansion of ERT personnel on the grounds of the White House with an expansion of the number of Counter-Sniper Team personnel assigned to watch the skies and the surrounding buildings around the White House and an expansion of the number of K-9 units around the eighteen-acre complex, then a terrorist assault team even considering an attack on the White House had better factor in massive casualties on their part first.

4. The Secret Service should double the special agent personnel assigned to evening and overnight shifts on the PPD when the president is "in residence." An organized terrorist tactical assault on the White House is likely to happen in the evening hours, when the enemy can take advantage of the low-light conditions and the inescapable physical fatigue that accompanies overnight work. Relatively simple changes to the special agent work schedule, combined with a substantial increase in the number of special agents assigned to the PPD (which is more likely to happen if the Secret Service forfeits some of its current investigative responsibilities and frees up a portion of its workforce for reassignment to the PPD) would allow the PPD to shorten overnight shift posting requirements by increasing the number of agents available for relief and tactical support in the event of an attack. Overnight shifts are also an ideal time for agents on their down time to familiarize themselves with the unbelievably complex White House grounds. To stay alert on overnight shifts at the White House when I was assigned to the PPD, I would walk the grounds, open doors I had never seen before, peek behind pillars in the Rose Garden, and generally familiarize myself with all of the hidden details of the White House. (The White House is full of surprises, and not everything a person sees at the White House is as it seems, even for tourists on the East and West Wing tours.) Increasing the number of agents on evening and overnight shifts would give the PPD agents a number of golden opportunities to create mental maps of the complicated layout of the White House. This would turn complexity into a tactical advantage for PPD agents familiar with the cover

and concealments options around the White House, rather than a hindrance, as it was on the night Jonathan Tran scaled multiple fences on the White House and Treasury complex grounds, and remained undetected for seventeen minutes.

5. The Secret Service should take advantage of the presidential travel schedule and occasionally use the White House during out-of-town trips for training exercises. The White House is a complex building with a labyrinthine interior. Expecting the special agents of the PPD and the Uniformed Division officers to respond in a manner tactically suitable enough to repel an organized terrorist assault team, while simultaneously preventing them from rehearsing the response to an attack on the actual White House grounds, is both illogical and dangerous. And although building a replica White House at the Secret Service training center in Maryland, for training purposes, was briefly proposed in 2015,[1] there was little legislative support on Capitol Hill for the multimillion-dollar expenditure. But there's no replacement for the real thing. And no replica White House, however realistic, can provide the valuable training experience that training exercises conducted on the White House grounds would provide. There are, however, some complications to using the White House for training. The Secret Service would have to close the north and south fence lines for the training to prevent the public, and potential adversaries, from taking note of their training response to specific simulated emergencies. Also, the White House staff members left behind to work at the White House while the president travels out of town would be slightly inconvenienced. But, the experience of repeatedly navigating around the actual White House grounds during stress-inducing training exercises, under simulated emergency conditions, would lend the Secret Service White House personnel an incredible tactical advantage in a firefight. There is no substitute for knowing your terrain better than your adversary, and training at the White House is the only way to build this body of tactical knowledge.

The Secret Service, despite its many organizational difficulties, can reestablish security dominance at the White House. And while the list of changes I proposed is by no means exhaustive, it's a small, but positive, start towards a more stable security arrangement at the White House. The country cannot afford a second-rate security plan in a first-rate threat environment. The terrorists are surely planning, as you read this, to hit us at the White House and it's incumbent on the Secret Service to hit back with a fury.

11

THE BROKEN SECRET SERVICE HIRING AND PROMOTION PROCESS

THERE ARE FEW THINGS WASHINGTON, DC, politicians and entrenched bureaucrats agree on. The 1980s ushered in a new era of electoral competition between the Democrats and the Republicans (before then the Democrats were the majority political party in both the House of Representatives and the Senate for most of the post–World War II era, while the Republicans had adopted a mostly "play-nice" strategy to stay politically relevant), and with that new competition for majority party status came increased political belligerency toward the opposing party when they were in power. But even with political tensions currently at redline levels, you would be hard-pressed to find any member of the

House or the Senate of either political party who would question the need to secure the life of the president of the United States. The gravity of the Secret Service's protection mission transcends politics and is understood by both partisan and nonpartisan actors to be critical to the survival of our constitutional republic. With a mission so recognizably vital to our nation's survival, one would think that the screening and hiring of candidates to conduct the protection mission would be agenda-free. A reasonable observer would expect that candidates for Secret Service agent and Uniformed Division officer employment and promotion would be judged exclusively by their ability to implement the protection mission and secure the life of the president. Unfortunately, if you choose to believe this, then you choose to be dead wrong.

Sadly, and for many years, the Secret Service has been sacrificing mission-readiness at the altar of political correctness. I hesitated to include this chapter because whenever someone mentions the term "diversity" and discusses the real-world implications of applying such a loosely defined term to a specific job description, he or she runs the severe risk of character assassination by extreme partisan actors who don't care a bit about the real-world ramifications of their ideological crusades. But the issue has become so serious in the Secret Service that it warrants discussing in the hope of providing enough public pressure to change this potentially disastrous policy. The Secret Service has a troubling fascination with informal, but no less real, gender and racial quotas in its hiring and promotion process, which is causing a growing tide of animosity to ripple across the agency. The subject is taboo to discuss in the polite company of Secret Service management, and they will assuredly deny this publicly if questioned about it, but it is a genuine problem. And if rank-and-file agents were given the opportunity to speak about the impact on the Secret Service of this obsession with racial and gender quotas without fear of retribution, many of them would tell a troubling tale. I know this because I lived it, and I spoke with agents during my career from different races and genders who felt that this problem was destructive to agency morale.

Although it's difficult to pinpoint exactly when the Secret Service management committed, above all else, to gender and racial quotas in promotion and hiring, I first noticed it in the early 2000s while assigned to the Long Island, New York, Secret Service office, where one of my assignments was recruiting and conducting background investigations for new special agent and Uniformed Division officer applicants. The same pattern would play out repeatedly in recruiting, where a small number of applicants with questionable job experience and qualifications (according to the Secret Service's own hiring standards) were expedited along in the hiring process because they were non-male, nonwhite applicants. This was troubling because, as I experienced firsthand later on in my career while assigned as an instructor in our Secret Service training academy, the results of some of these quota-driven hiring decisions in training exercises were disturbing. (Note: As a Secret Service recruiter, a background investigator, an agent, and an instructor for the Secret Service training academy, I saw the hiring process from inception to swearing-in. There was no good reason for gender and racial hiring quotas. My experience in the hiring process, and in observing the promotion process as an agent, was that there were more than enough skilled, and qualified people, regardless of race or gender, to both hire and promote into leadership positions in the Secret Service, but the Secret Service management simply decided to take the easy way out and quietly insist on quotas instead.)

The Secret Service's attachment to quota-based hiring was so intense that they hired applicants for the special agent and Uniformed Division officer positions that could barely meet basic physical fitness standards upon their commissioning as agents or officers. Some of these recruits for the special agent and officer positions were hired despite being unable to pull their own bodies up to a bar during a standard chin-up test. It was troubling for me, and many of my fellow agent and officer training-staff members assigned to the academy, to watch a fully grown adult, professing to want to be a member of the world's most elite protection force, struggle to do one single chin-up. This is not a matter of personal fitness choices, or of unnecessary attention to one component of the Secret Service physical training regimen. It's a matter of national security. If you are a Secret Service special agent or an officer, and you are on duty when a catastrophic assault occurs on the White House grounds, or when an attack on the president occurs, and you're the one closest to the president when he trips and falls in the evacuation and you can't muster the physical strength to lift him and carry him to safety, then it's not your fault if the president is hurt. This is the Secret Service's fault for hiring someone so completely incapable of carrying out its most basic mission requirements.

Doubly frightening is that these cases were not isolated. During my twelve years with the Secret Service, there were numerous cases of individuals on both the special agent and officer, sides of the Secret Service who were moved along in the hiring and training process despite having skills deficits that would unquestionably endanger the president if one of these individuals were to be charged with his security on a shift. Instructors at the Secret Service academy who called attention to these insurmountable physical-skills deficits in the agent trainees, hired based on a quota, were often either directly told, or indirectly hinted at, to "let it go." I know of one specific instructor, an exceptionally talented special agent and instructor, who was held back from coordinating new agent-trainee classes specifically because he was brutally honest in his evaluations of agent and officer trainees and the instructor refused to "let it go."

The coddling of people hired to fit the Secret Service's quotas, disturbingly, didn't end with the overlooking of glaring physical fitness deficiencies among their trainees. Many of the unqualified trainees who could barely perform one single chin-up, were also tactically deficient in the AOP exercises. AOP (Assault on Principal) exercises were training exercises where the trainees are placed in simulated protection roles as presidential protection shift members. These trainees are then put through a series of exercises, such as mock assassination attempts on the president. These exercises are often conducted using the Simunition ammunition, which I discussed earlier in the book, to impart a dose of realism. Simunition rounds fire via modified training weapons with smaller barrels (to prevent real weapons from being mixed in with Simunition weapons), and the plastic rounds contain a colored filler, similar to a paint ball. We would give one color Simunition round to the trainees and another color Simunition round to the instructors so the training staff could evaluate, at the conclusion of the exercise, who fired at, and hit, whom. The benefit of training with the Simunition rounds was the intense pain—and welts—they caused when you were hit. The threat of being hit by a Simunition round brought real fear into the training exercise, and there is no coach as good as pain and fear to teach a trainee to fight back furiously.

The AOP exercises using the Simunition rounds were always the exercises where the cream would rise to the top. Regretfully, I was never a member of our U.S. military. But I was always proud to watch these AOP exercises as an instructor and to witness our former military members, who were now Secret Service trainees, calmly, and with precision, neutralize a threat in an AOP exercise without ever "shitting the bed" (see chapter 9). Without being told in advance who the former military members were, it was clear to me within seconds of the gunshots ringing out in these exercises who the military veterans were. Our military does an incredible job training our fighting men and women to operate cleanly in the "red zone" (the fight in the "fight or flight" response, where the heart rate increases and precise motor activities are difficult), and it was always refreshing to see them excel in Secret Service training while serving as mentors for otherwise competent trainees who were struggling because they had never been immersed in exercises using simulated battle-stress conditions. However, the competency of the military veterans in the training exercises served as a dramatic foil to the incompetency of some of the trainees hired based primarily on quotas. Some of the same trainees who struggled to meet the basic trainee physical fitness requirements also struggled to effectively mount any significant resistance during AOP exercises. Many would struggle to fight back, others would fire their weapons indiscriminately, and at times, some would hinder the team's ability to evacuate the protectee during the exercises. Some would even accidentally shoot, and hit, their fellow trainees with one of their Simunition rounds during the more intense exercises (if the trainees were given red Simunition rounds, and a trainee had a red Simunition spot on his or her back, then it was clear that another trainee had fired that shot). This was all deeply disturbing to the other trainees who witnessed the physical fitness shortcomings and the tactical ineffectiveness of many of the questionable hires, and it was devastating to trainee morale. Many of the trainees felt as if there were two evaluation systems in the training academy: one for white male agents and another for quota-based hires. Again, I understand that this information may disturb many of you, and that it may rile up extreme left-wing partisans, who've convinced themselves that checking a series of race-based and gender-based boxes is all that really matters in the world, but this quota-based policy had crushing effects on the people charged with keeping our president safe. Ignoring this in order to engage in an ongoing game of political correctness will do nothing to fix the Secret Service.

Halfway through my tenure as an instructor in the training academy, I was told by an upper-level manager assigned to the academy that one student, who was having extreme difficulty meeting performance standards on any of the physical or tactical exercises, was to be "left alone" because the trainee "knew the system." This manager was referring to the Equal Employment Opportunity complaint system, and appeared to fear a baseless EEO complaint more than harming a protectee by graduating an unqualified trainee. It was an eye-opening moment for me, and another example of the federal government working against its own interests in order to advance politically correct ideas. The federal government doesn't have anxious stockholders or customers to please in the traditional sense. The government takes your money, using the threat of force to back it up through the IRS, and they spend it on whatever they choose. And as long as the political insider class continues to get reelected, they will continue to ignore festering problems by allowing agencies such as the Secret Service to push through incompetent trainees, who are putting the president and other Secret Service protectees in very real danger. Unlike the private sector, where angry stockholders or customers can force a company to change or they'll lose their business, few people are ever held to account in the federal government, even when dangerous policies, such as choosing hiring quotas over competence, are allowed to continue.

A repeated theme of this book has been Secret Service management's fear of controversy, and their corresponding risk-aversion, when it means confronting brewing crises. The push to evaluate trainees, at least in part, according to their race or gender, rather than strictly on their qualifications for the job, was an unfortunate example of this reluctance to do the right thing. Secret Service management fears charges of bias and discrimination, and they will do nearly anything to avoid them. This pattern repeats itself and ripples across an agent's or an officer's career, and it is destroying the agency from the inside out. Everything from an agent's or officer's initial assignment, to his or her selection for a special team (the Emergency Response Team, the K-9 Team, the Counter-Sniper Team, the Presidential Protective Division, and more) is influenced by the Secret Service's obsession with the racial and gender quota system, and nearly everyone in the Secret Service knows it. One tragic outcome from this ill-advised and misguided policy is that many high-performing nonwhite, female agents and officers have privately expressed to me sincere reservations about this quota system, because they feel that they will never be respected for their job skills. Many of the agents and officers view the under-performing employees, shielded from negative job action by a fear of baseless EEO discrimination claims, as a burden to the Secret Service. One of these agents, known throughout the agency as an exceptional performer, and who was a "triple threat" (Secret Service jargon for looking the part, acting the part, and talking the part), expressed to me many times the grave concerns he had with quota-based hires being placed in critical assignments close to the president. Many of the quota-based hires were not only pushed through the

Secret Service academy, but they were also prioritized in their career development and placed in hard-to-get assignments, such as the PPD, despite having severe deficiencies in their abilities to perform the tasks necessary to secure the life of the president, and this agent knew it. The agent once said something to me, referring to a quota-based hire, that stuck with me: "_____ is going to get someone killed one day." I never forgot that. And as someone concerned about the safety and security of the president of the United States, you shouldn't either.

PART 2

WHAT THE SECRET SERVICE IS DOING RIGHT

12

THE SPECIAL AGENT TRAINING PROGRAM

WHEN I GRADUATED the Secret Service agent training program in December 1999, the training curriculum was archaic. The training program is broken into four general parts: academics, physical fitness, firearms, and control tactics. The academic portion of the training program was designed to teach agent trainees how to navigate and apply federal laws, how to properly investigate protectee threat cases, how to apply investigative tools to investigate financial crimes and counterfeit currency cases, and how to apply federal statutes and Secret Service guidelines to the design and implementation of a properly designed protectee security plan. The physical fitness portion of the training program was designed to prepare incoming agents for the intense physical demands necessary to repel an attack on the president. The firearms training program was designed to teach agent-trainees how to operate the Sig Sauer service pistol, issued to all agents, the Heckler and Koch MP-5 machine gun (used primarily in support of the protection mission, but also available for law enforcement operations), and the Remington 870 shotgun (used for breaching doors in the protection mission, but primarily used for law enforcement operations). The control tactics portion of the program was designed to teach agent trainees the most effective hand-to-hand combat techniques for use in both the protection and law enforcement missions. The problem when I went through the training academy in 1999 was that portions of the curriculum at the time did very little to actually advance these training goals.

The academic curriculum in 1999 was unfocused and antiquated. It was written as a series of case studies of investigations, but the material was dated, and it didn't reflect current investigative trends. It emphasized process (mainly administrative paperwork requirements) at the expense of advanced instruction for the agent trainees on how to properly use and apply investigative tools to solve a federal criminal case. For example, the surveillance exercise, which was obviously supposed to teach agent-trainees how to surveil a criminal suspect, was little more than an exercise in following a Secret Service staff instructor around the Annapolis waterfront while he or she shopped for cigars or clothes. I remember thinking to myself during the exercise how majestic the views were from the dock in downtown Annapolis, as I stared at an instructor pretending to be a criminal suspect (while he was also pretending not to notice me). More important, I was also thinking, *What the hell are we doing here?* Following a pretend "bad guy" around Annapolis, while we both pretend not to recognize each other, with little hard instruction on the proper way to conduct surveillance was a microcosm of most of the academic portion of the training program in 1999. If you asked the dreaded "Why are we doing this?" question about much of the academic portion of the training program, you would get a similar answer, despite learning little about how to be a criminal investigator: "Because that's the way we've always done it."

The control tactics training wasn't much better and it left trainees ill prepared for a physical confrontation. The Secret Service was teaching its agents and officers a modified version of aikido and traditional Japanese jiu-jitsu, which it called "Desmonics," after the instructor who developed the program years prior. The program was a failure by modern standards of hand-to-hand combat science and mainly taught students how to roll and fall properly without smashing their heads into the concrete. But aikido-type techniques, while potentially street-usable after decades of training, are virtually useless in a law enforcement academy with just hours of instruction a week for just a few months. However, the program was good for comic relief in the stressful training environment. There were some incredibly athletic and accomplished agents in my training class who excelled at firearms training, academics, and in the tactical exercises, but some of them could not figure out, regardless of how many times they tried, how to forward roll the "Desmonics" way. It became an exercise in laughter control, not control tactics, each time we would start the class with a series of forward rolls on the heavily padded, law-enforcement-blue floor of the control tactics building, and the forward roll–challenged students would plunge themselves facefirst into the mats. They would get up and slap themselves in disapproval as we all tried our hardest not to laugh. We all knew it wasn't funny watching these trainees struggle with this senseless technique, but it's an almost undeniable human instinct to laugh when someone literally jumps into what he or she thinks is going to be a graceful aikido roll, and it winds up morphing into a belly flop into a waterless pool. Humor aside, this was a silly and unnecessary training regime. The essence of law enforcement focused hand-to-hand combat techniques is to learn to control a suspect until you can either handcuff him, or control him physically until help arrives. The goal is not to teach the agents to be professional stunt performers or Golden Gloves boxers. But that's exactly what the program was trying to do.

The control tactics boxing program was even more counterproductive. When we weren't learning how to roll around on the floor, we were learning how to box. Teaching basic boxing techniques to law enforcement trainees may sound sensible, but it isn't. If you approach a suspect for an interview, or in an arrest situation, and the suspect assumes a boxing or fighting stance, then an armed law enforcement officer should supersede this level of force by the degree necessary to overcome it. The law enforcement officer or agent has no legal obligation whatsoever to match the level of force first, before superseding it. For example, if a suspect takes a fighting stance and becomes physically aggressive, the Secret Service, along with most other law enforcement agencies' use-of-force guidelines, allows agents to use their hand-held extendible batons to fight back. The use-of-force guidelines, for common-sense reasons, do not require an agent to engage in a prolonged hand-to-hand boxing match before taking out his or her baton to use in self-defense. Another example would be a suspect attacking an agent with a knife during an altercation. The use-of-force guidelines allow an agent in this deadly-force scenario to immediately use his or her firearm to diffuse the situation and to stop the deadly attack against him. Again, the agent is not required to first match the force level by engaging the suspect in a knife fight. This seems to have escaped the early designers of the control tactics training program, who spent inordinate amounts of control-tactics class time on teaching agents how to box. I struggled at the time to think of a good reason to teach this incredibly difficult skill to law enforcement officers. I was a boxer at the time, and I trained at a gym called Knockout Fitness, and I couldn't help but think, *I've been at this boxing thing for years, and I'm still not very good at it.* Yet, the instructional program designers thought they could train the agent trainees to be street-effective boxers in a few months? It was backwards thinking. Worse, as the training program came to a close, they would have the trainees spar with each other. This was an incredibly irresponsible approach to hand-to-hand combat training. No credible boxing trainer would allow even a junior boxer into the ring for sparring sessions without mastering the basics first, yet, the trainees, with zero experience ever being hit, or hitting someone else, were told to give it a go. Yes, the results were exactly what you would expect. It wasn't uncommon for trainees to get knocked out cold, or for some to go to the hospital. Imagine for a moment what it must be like for an agent trainee who has never even sniffed a fistfight, much less been in one, to be thrust into a sparring exercise with a stone-cold, seasoned streetfighter trainee who has knocked out more people in the street than Mike Tyson in the ring. These scenarios never ended well. All the agent trainee with no sparring experience learned in this scenario was how to get his or her ass kicked with dignity, and what smelling salts look like up close and personal.

The physical fitness training in the late '90s was a bright spot for the Secret Service. Between the obstacle course, the weight room, and the sprint work around the training center grounds, the physical fitness program produced decent results. The Secret Service fitness instructors wouldn't hesitate back then to yell at, and kick some dirt on, the trainees if the effort they were putting forth wasn't optimal. This military-style fitness training gave many of the new trainees an edge. There's a reason training academies and military boot camps looking to imbue their trainees with a mental edge use stress and discomfort in their training programs. The act of yelling at and causing both emotional and physical discomfort for trainees places them in the physiological red zone. Learning to operate and carry out the Secret Service protection mission with your heart racing and your lungs screaming for air, while being screamed at and pushed to your physical limit, was the primary focus of the fitness program, and the instructors carried out the mission with laser-like precision.

The firearms training during my time as an agent trainee was outstanding. When I joined the Secret Service, I was already familiar with firearms due to my training as a New York City police officer, but I was pleasantly surprised to see that the Secret Service had a different outlook on firearms training. The NYPD firearms training taught firearms competency, not firearms excellence, but the Secret Service didn't have that luxury. Granted, the logistics were not in the NYPD's favor, as their police academy classes could number in the thousands of new police recruits, while the Secret Service had a maximum of less than fifty trainees per class. But the Secret Service had no room for error. They drilled into us from day one of training that we were "accountable for every round" fired from our pistols. This may seem obvious in a law enforcement training academy, but it meant a lot more to the Secret Service. The Secret Service places men and women just inches away from the president of the United States, and, in the unfortunate circumstance that a firearm has to be used to defend the president, it must be done with extreme precision and barrel discipline. Firing a weapon in an exchange of gunfire in an altercation on an empty street with a hardened criminal is a far different scenario from firing a weapon at a crowded event, with tens of thousands of people, on a rope line, and with the president inches from your weapon. And while the concern for innocent bystanders is no different for a local police officer or a Secret Service agent the environments they are likely to encounter during a deadly-force interaction are far different. There is virtually no scenario a Secret Service agent in a protective capacity will encounter where there aren't hundreds, or thousands, of innocent bystanders surrounding the agent. It's a natural part of protecting the most targeted human being in the world; therefore, precision shooting is critical.

One of the pistol that we as new agent trainees had to pass in the initial weeks of training was designed to teach this critical firearms discipline. The course sounds easy, but skilled shooters from both police departments and the military would routinely come up short on the course, having to shoot the course multiple times in order to pass. The course of fire was from the standing position, with the target fifteen yards away from the shooter. You were given nearly unlimited time to shoot the course, but the target was no larger than a small microwave pizza, and just a few misses outside of the bullseye of the target was enough to fail. Maybe it was the extended timeline that caused most of us to stress out over each round, but I recall bringing my Sig Sauer issued firearm up to eye level to place the shot three or four times before actually firing the first shot. Looking to the left and right of me, it was clear that my fellow agent trainees were doing the same thing, as the clear lack of a restrictive time limit on the training course made us all hyperattentive to each detail of the upcoming shot. And while this course was designed to be more of a test of the psychological component to shooting than the physical component, the other firearms courses were designed to test our tactical abilities to shoot the shotgun, MP-5 machine gun, and pistol under pressure. Some of the courses required us to sprint about two hundred yards from the fitness facility on the training campus to the outdoor range, and to then pick up a series of firearms while engaging moving targets, all while firearms instructors were screaming in our ears. Although the targets were paper, they were on a horizontal track, which allowed them to move rapidly from side to side. Complicating the course of fire was the placement of "friendly" targets (targets that pictured civilians without weapons) placed strategically along the horizontal track. If you hit them as you tracked and fired at the "bad guy" target, you would fail the course of fire. Doing all of this while sucking wind through our lungs because we'd just sprinted two hundred yards to the range was difficult, but it drove home for many of us the difficulties of firing at, and hitting, a target at a distance, while physiologically operating in the physiological red zone during an attack on the president.

Their commitment to fixing the shortcomings of the training program, unlike some of the other managerial deficiencies within the Secret Service, was impressive. I was assigned to the New York field office protective intelligence squad in the early 2000s when I saw a special agent job opening in the James J. Rowley Training Center for a control tactics instructor. I only had a few years of experience as an agent at the time, but I inquired about the position. I found out that the training staff at the training center were looking for someone from the field office to transfer to the training center who had experience in ground fighting and Brazilian jiu-jitsu. At the time, I was training in a ground fighting school in Long Island, New York, and I was one of the few applicants for this position who had the experience they were looking for. The Secret Service was prescient in seeing the need for this type of training in the early 2000s, as most law enforcement academies were still teaching boxing as their primary form of hand-to-hand combat training. But the explosive growth of the Ultimate Fighting Championship, and the corresponding growth in the number of ground fighting and Brazilian jiu-jitsu schools around the country, garnered the attention of instructors in the Secret Service academy. As a result, they were eager to begin the transition from boxing to ground fighting. This move made sense from a practical perspective. If a suspect takes a fighting stance in an altercation with an agent, then the agent is trained to move up the force continuum until the subject is subdued, not to get involved in a boxing match. But if an agent is attempting to arrest a suspect, and the suspect tackles the agent, opportunity is limited to take out a baton or firearm to fight back. The decision to move away from boxing, and to train agents to fight back using ground-based fighting techniques inspired by Brazilian jiu-jitsu, was a brilliant move that has paid enormous dividends. Many of the instructors, inspired by the effectiveness of the ground fighting training, eventually took up training outside of the workday and have subsequently passed on their newfound expertise to the later Secret Service trainees. The training staff even had a Wednesday night "fight club" training session, after hours in the basement mat room of the training center, where I and members of the training staff would get together and basically beat the crap out of each other while fine-tuning the latest ground fighting techniques. These Wednesday fight club sessions were invaluable. I learned more in those marathon ground fighting sessions in the fight club than I did in years of training outside of the training center.

The management staff at the training center took this open-minded approach to the redesign of the control tactics program, and to their credit, they applied it to other components of the training program as well. The academic training in investigative tactics was clearly broken at the time. It used outdated case studies that only taught agent trainees what the agent who had worked the case ten-plus years ago had done—even if he or she had done it wrong. Although I was transferred to the training center to teach in the control tactics section, I only spent a few weeks there. The investigative tactics section was short instructors at the time, and I agreed to temporarily fill in there to ease the manpower strain. The temporary assignment quickly turned permanent when the supervisor of the section and I hit it off.

"Don" was an excellent supervisor who had served as an agent in the Vice Presidential Protective Division agent, but he never held a grudge about it. There was always a healthy tension between the PPD agents and the VPPD agents, mainly because the PPD was considered the "A-Team" within the Secret Service, and the available spots there were limited. As a result of the limited openings, a number of qualified agents hoping to be assigned to the PPD were forced over to the VPPD, and some remained bitter about it, even years later. That was unfortunate because some of the best agents I worked with during my tenure with the Secret Service were VPPD agents. The VPPD agents had an expression, "We do more, with less," and they were correct. The threat level to the vice president isn't that much different from that of the president, yet the VPPD agents were always struggling in the fight for limited protection assets. Whether it was magnetometers, Uniformed Division officers, or "post-standers" (special agents not assigned to the PPD or VPPD, but taken from the field offices to support the protection mission), they were always fighting with headquarters to get the assets they needed to accomplish the mission. This constant struggle for assets forced the VPPD agents to be extra creative when designing their security plans, and it showed when many of them were later promoted because they carried over much of this creativity and "outside the box" thinking to their new managerial assignments. The tension between the protective details still remained, though, as some of the agents on the PPD when I was there would joke around and say, "No one comes to the Secret Service to protect number two," referring to the vice president. Don was one of those former VPPD agents who took his creativity with him from the VPPD to his new supervisory position in the training center's investigative tactics section. He had a meeting with the special agents assigned to the section early in my tenure there, and he was clear that we were going to redesign and rewrite everything. But instead of updating the antiquated case studies, Don decided that we were going to do it right. We were going to abandon the case-study approach in the investigative tactics section and instead teach the agent trainees how to be the best federal investigators in the country. But to do that, we had a good bit of learning to do ourselves.

Most of the agents assigned to the investigative tactics section as instructors, like me, were relatively new to the agency, and we were "pre-detail" (newer agents who hadn't yet completed a full-time protection assignment); therefore, our collective experience was limited. To overcome this skills deficit, along with the deficits in the training program, we undertook a bold initiative to reach out to the federal, state, and local law enforcement agencies that had a reputation for excellence in specific investigative tactics, and ask them for help. Not knowing where to start, a few of us began cold-calling agencies such as the Drug Enforcement Administration (DEA) and some of the federal government's intelligence agencies, and asking them if we could sit in on their training. It took a few rounds of follow-up phone calls to get to the decision makers, but thankfully, a number of the agencies were gracious and agreed to either let us attend their academies or to assist us themselves in redesigning our own training program.

Two standout agencies who contributed greatly to this effort were the DEA and the military intelligence community. The DEA has a body of experience in undercover operations second to none. Their agents are constantly putting themselves in severe danger by going undercover to buy illegal drugs and contraband in order to further their investigations, and one small mistake could quickly cost them their lives. When the DEA agents agreed to join us at the Secret Service academy to train us, the instructors, they brought with them a series of disturbing videos of undercover operations "gone bad" because of avoidable mistakes. It was admirable that the DEA agents had embraced some of the mistakes they made in the past as an agency, and used them as training tools and cautionary tales for others engaged in dangerous undercover work. The Secret Service does the same thing when it trains outside agencies in protection operations by using the John F. Kennedy and Ronald Reagan attacks as examples of what *not* to do.

The videos were tough to watch. One specific video showed the outside of a house where an undercover operator was conducting a drug buy inside. In the middle of the operation, a coconspirator who was hiding in closet leaped out, and both suspects attempted to rip off the undercover officer. The criminals didn't know the undercover operator was law enforcement. They thought they were ripping off another criminal drug dealer. The audio of the altercation from the undercover operator's body wire is tough to listen to. Knowing he had children and was beaten within inches of his life was a rude awakening to just how dangerous undercover operations are. When the video ended, we were all dead silent. Not a word was said. Our stares did all the speaking, saying, *Did that just happen?* It reminded us all about how irresponsible it is to teach subpar tactics to agents who could be endangered by them. Candidly, we had been teaching little about tactics and a lot about paperwork and administrative processes, when in the real world, it's bad tactics that could get our agent-trainees killed or injured, leaving their children without parents. We were so focused on the administrative paperwork process in the training program that we lost the forest for the trees. It's really not that big of a deal when an agent forgets to sign an evidence analysis request to the Secret Service Forensic Services Division. Paperwork mistakes can be corrected, but mistakes in a dangerous undercover operation can easily kill you. What we were committed to caring about after the undercover videos was teaching agent trainees to stay alive. The paperwork is easy in the Secret Service, and relatively self-explanatory; we weren't asking trainees to analyze the quarterly cash-flow statements for IBM. Besides, wasting precious training time teaching agent trainees to fill out paperwork, when they could take the information back with them at night and go over it on their own time, made this old approach to training look that much more foolish. Teaching the agent trainees world-class investigative tactics was clearly the more productive path to creating world-class criminal investigators.

After the DEA "train the trainer" undercover course, I, along with the rest of the instructor staff, felt invigorated. With a sense of purpose, we deconstructed the entire Secret Service undercover tactics training program and incorporated the world-class tactics taught to us by the DEA experts. But we didn't stop at undercover tactics; we went on to scrap the interviewing and interrogation portions of the training program, along with the surveillance training program, rebuilding those programs using the most advanced and modern techniques. A friend and coworker of mine in the investigative tactics section took on the interviewing and interrogation portion and began to research better ways to teach the agent trainees these valuable skills. I took on the surveillance program.

The interview and interrogation training at the time, although it needed an upgrade, was in decent shape. Due to the Secret Service's critical protective intelligence mission, which required them to interview people who threatened their protectees on a recurring basis, the training was relatively up-to-date. The Secret Service management never forgot the devastating lessons of the attempted assassination of President Gerald Ford by Sara Jane Moore, and this incident impacted their outlook toward modernizing the interviewing and interrogation training. Secret Service agents had interviewed Moore before her 1975 assassination attempt of Ford, where she fired a shot at President Ford from a revolver during a presidential visit to San Francisco, California. The interviewing agents mistakenly determined that she was not an immediate threat. This devastating judgment error served as a cautionary tale in the Secret Service academy when I went through as an agent trainee, and again later in my career, when I returned as an instructor. Much of the interviewing course relied on techniques used by a private company that specialized in interviewing and interrogation. This company taught their techniques to various entities in the intelligence, law enforcement, and corporate worlds, and they were well respected in the law enforcement and intelligence communities for their training product. Their interviewing and interrogation techniques were clever, and I learned to use some of them in other areas of my life outside of my special agent career. They taught us how to follow the direction of the eyes of the suspects we were interviewing. If they looked upwards, and in a specific direction, it could be an indicator of deception. They also taught us the "rule of threes," which was a tool for getting a confession out of a suspect when you're reasonably sure about the nature and degree of the crime. In other words, if you know a suspect printed and passed $100 in counterfeit money, then during the interrogation you can say to the suspect, "We know you printed the $300 in counterfeit," multiplying the actual amount by three. And if you're convincing enough, some of the suspects will come back with, "*Three* hundred? I only printed *one* hundred." You may chuckle, but the technique works pretty well, and I used it successfully a number of times in financial crimes investigations. It was these techniques, combined with new material, and an emphasis on redesigning the associated practical exercises, where the students would interview a trained actor playing a criminal suspect, that eventually replaced the outdated case-study-based classes.

Unfortunately, the surveillance program was a total disaster, and I was committed to scrapping the entire program. It was nothing more than an exercise in following people around. That's not surveillance; it's stalking, and it requires no special set of skills to do. However, professional surveillance does require intense training. It's a complicated exercise in seeing others without being seen yourself. I had to search for a while to find an agency willing to teach us how to do surveillance, but upon advice from a coworker (the same one who rewrote the interviewing course), I settled on approaching a group of former military intelligence experts and asking them for their help. These guys were top-tier and had conducted surveillance in some of the most dangerous countries in the world for American operators to work in. If they made a surveillance mistake, and they were "burned" (discovered by the person they were surveilling), they could wind up arrested, beaten, or worse. The penalties for these men for surveillance mistakes were very real, and their techniques were light-years ahead of the "Hey, go follow the instructor to Annapolis" surveillance class we painfully suffered through when I was a student in the Secret Service academy. They taught us surveillance techniques ranging from using "hazards" (forks and turns in the roads) to your advantage when surveilling a suspect, to avoiding "dough boys" (innocent civilians who notice you surveilling the target, and who inform the suspect that he's being watched). They even had clever terms for suspects who would speed up in a vehicle surveillance to get through yellow traffic lights, to leave a surveillance team in the dust. They called this "squeezing the lemon." But they also taught us valuable techniques for detecting surveillance on ourselves. Learning how to detect surveillance on ourselves was a skill that would come in handy later in my career on presidential protection when I was in the transportation section of the PPD and would escort the presidential vehicles from the military planes they flew in on back to the secure hotel. It always helped to use those countersurveillance skills to ensure that we weren't being followed by hostile elements looking to see where we stashed the secure presidential vehicle package. The golden rule of countersurveillance was time, distance, and direction. If you're followed for a long period of *time*, it doesn't necessarily mean you're being surveilled, because the person following you may be going to the same place you're going. If you're followed for a long *distance* by the same person, it may be suspicious, but again, maybe the driver is going to the same location. But if you incorporate some changes in direction and the person is still following you, now it's time to heighten your suspicion. The course was far more complicated than this oversimplification, but I was proud to update the training program to reflect the advice and training techniques of these former military experts.

My experience in helping redesign the Secret Service's training program taught me what can be done when the current alphabet soup of federal agencies combines efforts and expertise to produce a better product for the taxpayers. And given our disastrous national debt, it only makes sense in the future for federal lawmakers, and the president, to be visionary and to look at a complete reorganization of the current federal law enforcement and intelligence bureaucracy. Dividing up the federal law enforcement and intelligence responsibilities among an alphabet soup of federal agencies may have made sense to lawmakers in the past who were concerned about the power of a single federal police force. But as we saw with the Susan Rice/Obama administration spying scandal, where White House officials requested the unmasking of the names of Trump associates being spied on by our government, abuses of power can happen even when responsibilities and power are divided among agencies. It's time we moved toward a single federal law enforcement agency, where expertise can be shared vertically and horizontally throughout the new organization; a single intelligence agency that can be strictly monitored by Congress and can share valuable intelligence seamlessly both vertically and horizontally; and a single internal affairs/inspector general, who could work with Congress to monitor the activities of the law enforcement and intelligence operations, to battle the inevitable creep toward power abuses.

13

INTERAGENCY COOPERATION

THE COOPERATION WITH OUTSIDE FEDERAL AGENCIES in the redesign and development of the new agent training program in 2002, 2003, and 2004 was an example of something the Secret Service, despite all of its recent problems, generally does very well: cooperation. Secret Service upper-level management found it difficult to institute systemic, agencywide changes until White House security breaches and other public agency failures increased public pressure to the point where the status quo was untenable; however, the working agents in both the field offices and on protective details, by necessity, have very good working relationships with outside law enforcement agencies. Seeking help from the DEA and military intelligence operators in the redesign of the agent-training program was natural for me and my coworkers in the investigative tactics section of the Secret Service training center because seeking help from outside agencies was an essential component of our jobs when we were special agents in the field offices. Even the most junior special agent in the field office figures out quickly that he or she cannot design a security plan for a Secret Service protectee without the help of local law enforcement.

When a special agent is designing a security plan to protect the president against threats from the "big-six" threats, he must keep manpower concerns in mind when designing the plan within the three rings of security, the outer, middle, and inner rings. For example, the innermost security perimeter, which is best described as the roughly arm's length area surrounding the president, is almost always manned exclusively by special agents from the Secret Service's PPD. With few exceptions, the Secret Service prefers to keep this inner ring staffed with its own agents because of the very specific protection training its agents go through. Secret Service agents are trained in the control tactics program how to remove the dreaded huggers and hand shakers from their protectees. In the inner ring agents deal with these problems often. People, most with no ill intent, can get overexcited in the presence of the president and other world leaders the Secret Service protects, and many of them will hug the protectees or vigorously shake their hands and, sometimes, refuse to let go. The Secret Service trains regularly on simple joint manipulations using the hands and elbows that will allow them to remove an overexcited hugger or hand shaker from a protectee. This training, along with the rope-line training, where agents are trained to focus their attention on a zone of coverage rather than on the protectee, and close quarters firearms training, where agents learn to use an extra level of muzzle discipline while working closely with the protectee, makes Secret Service agents ideally suited for the inner protection ring. The rare exception I've seen is when the president or a world leader travels to New York City. The NYPD was always terrific to work with, but they would always insist that one of their Intelligence Division detectives be allowed to work the inner ring with the Secret Service protective detail. Due to the different training and job requirements of the NYPD detectives in the Intelligence Division and the Secret Service agents working the inner ring, I never thought this was a good idea. (I successfully completed not only the New York City Police Academy, but also the Secret Service agent-training course and the Secret Service Protective Detail Training Course, and although the training is high-quality in all of these, it's different in preparing their officers and agents for their respective missions). But the Secret Service management in the New York field office and the management of the protective details never "big-leagued" (Secret Service jargon for cocky federal agents talking down to local police officers) the NYPD and tried to kick them out of the inner ring. I always admired the better managers in the Secret Service, and their desire to see the big picture, when circumstances presented them with a series of unpalatable options. Cooperation was key to the New York field office management staff when I worked there, and the management understood that the larger protection mission was better served by allowing an NYPD detective in the inner ring, despite some training disparities, rather than big-leaguing the detective and kicking him or her out, upsetting NYPD management, and destroying the generally positive feelings the two agencies had toward each other.

Learning to put your federal agent ego aside and to be a team player with the NYPD and local police departments around the country was an essential part of being an effective special agent.

The middle perimeter, which is the area a protectee will walk through and bypass during the course of an event, is mutually shared by the Secret Service and outside law enforcement agencies. Cooperation in this middle perimeter is essential, and a successful security plan absolutely requires the full buy-in of the cooperating law enforcement agencies while working within it. The Secret Service often uses "pipe and drape" to close off the sensitive areas of its protected sites from public view. But pipe and drape is not a physical barrier (it's literally a blue sheet hanging from a pipe); it's a visual barrier only. However, with the addition of outside law enforcement to complement Secret Service agents on the outside of the pipe and drape, you now have an effective deterrent to someone straying into your secure area. The Secret Service relies heavily on outside law enforcement in the middle perimeter because in the real world, outside of the training environment, it's completely impractical for a Secret Service agent to arrest someone for trespassing if he or she strays into the secure area. The arrest would pull the agent off of the posting assignment, and it would take hours of paperwork to process the arrest. The agent would probably be laughed out of federal court if he presented a case such as this to a federal prosecutor (these are such burdensome cases that the Secret Service will often rely on local prosecution even for trespassers at the White House, which, I believe, incentivizes more people to jump the fence because of the lack of a credible penalty). But the uniformed law enforcement officers in the middle perimeter, in addition to serving as a strong visual deterrent (the special agents of the Secret Service do not have uniforms), are vital because the officers can easily issue a trespass citation or, if necessary, make an arrest if someone intentionally enters the secure area, without getting bogged down in hours of federal paperwork.

The outer perimeter is primarily, but not excusively, manned by non–Secret Service law enforcement personnel and is typically the ring of security that is the most manpower-intensive. The outer perimeter consists of the motorcade route and the areas around protected sites, which require access control and "eyes on" (law enforcement–trained personnel to intercept vehicles and people attempting to circumvent the security fencing or temporary barriers). The Secret Service, due to its small size and geographically spread out field offices, does not have the manpower to provide a special agent for every post on the manpower-heavy outer perimeter. Therefore, cooperation with local law enforcement is critical in obtaining and deploying their equipment assets and manpower to ensure that the perimeter is fully staffed during a protection mission.

It's these critical soft skills, learning to request the appropriate assets and dealing respectfully with outside law enforcement agencies during the protection mission, that have always served the Secret Service well, while effective liaison remains a soft spot for some of the other federal law enforcement agencies. There is a tangible tension in many of America's big cities between some federal law enforcement agencies, notably ICE and the FBI, and the local law police departments. Some of this is due to the larger political environment, specifically with regard to ICE and the ongoing immigration debate, but some of this tension is due to jurisdictional turf battles, the lack of information sharing, and sometimes, just plain old "big-leaguing." The Secret Service doesn't have the option of starting fights with local law enforcement about petty jurisdictional fights or information sharing because the Secret Service cannot do its job without outside law enforcement help. Outside law enforcement provides the Secret Service with critical intelligence about local crime trends (an essential component of any protective intelligence advance in any of the locations the president or another protectee visits), stolen police uniforms (always a significant threat in the Secret Service because of the access they provide), and essential manpower to secure posts in the middle and outer perimeters. This forces junior agents to learn the soft skills necessary to gain cooperation from their local law enforcement partners, and it has given the Secret Service a generally strong reputation among the nation's law enforcement agencies. I still receive positive e-mails and social media connections from law enforcement officers across the country extolling the virtues of the Secret Service agents they worked with when the president or a world leader visited their city or town.

14

YOUR CHILD'S SCHOOL IS SAFER BECAUSE THE SECRET SERVICE STUDIED ASSASSINS

INVESTIGATING PEOPLE WHO THREATEN THE LIFE of the president of the United States, world leaders on U.S. soil, and the group of individuals the Secret Service is charged with protecting according to 18 U.S. Code section 3056 is unquestionably the most important mission the Secret Service has. There is no room for errors when conducting PI investigations. If a special agent interviews a PI subject who has threatened a Secret Service protectee and that agent determines that the subject presents no threat, then, after filing a long and laborious report with Secret Service headquarters (due to the seriousness of PI investigations, headquarters monitors every PI case and holds the investigating agent to a strict reporting timeline with little tolerance for reporting delays), the case is typically closed. If the subject then attempts to harm a Secret Service protectee, not only has the agent failed to execute his or her responsibility to properly assess the threat of the subject, but the Secret Service has failed as well in managing its primary responsibility, protectee safety. The importance of learning how to properly diagnose the danger level a PI subject presents after making a presidential threat is made crystal clear to Secret Service agents from the moment they swear in as new employees. A supervisory agent I respected for his candor once told me, "You can screw up a lot of things here, but you can't screw up a PI investigation."

Here is an incident I experienced that demonstrates the seriousness that Secret Service headquarters applies to PI cases. I was on duty in the New York field office protective intelligence squad on October 3, 2002, when Steve Kim fired multiple shots from a .357 caliber revolver at the upper floors of the United Nations building on the east side of Manhattan. When the news broke and our office was notified about the incident, we sent a friend of mine, an agent named Scott, out to investigate. Secret Service headquarters was all over this, and I remember the immediate chaos in the office as headquarters repeatedly called the backup (the agent immediately in line to the supervisor of the field office squad) and wanted answers regarding the shooter's intent. During the early stages of an event such as this, intent can be tough to determine, and if it weren't for the leaflets that the shooter had with him regarding the plight of the North Koreans, then the investigation into motive and intent could have taken a while. In this case, the shooter's intent was relatively clear, but the immediate search for answers, as evidenced by the constant calls from headquarters, is an example of the gravity of a PI case and the pressure to produce immediate answers. Secret Service headquarters was concerned that the shooter was targeting a Secret Service protectee, and if that were the case, they would have demanded access to Kim early on in the arrest and interview process to assess the threat level. Immediate questions such as "Did you act alone?"; "Where did you acquire the weapon?"; "Have you communicated with a Secret Service protectee before?"; and "Did you have any additional plans?" would have been critical questions if Kim were determined to be a threat to a Secret Service protectee.

The Secret Service has long been recognized for its expertise in assessing the threat level of the many subjects that it comes into contact with each year for threatening their protectees. Threats are reported to the Secret Service in many ways, and I witnessed the evolution of the reporting process during my time as a special agent. When I first joined the Secret Service as an agent in 1999, most of the tips for PI cases came in via telephone to the field offices. It was pretty common for a bartender to call into the office and notify us that a drunken bar patron has said that he wanted to "hurt the president," or worse. But tips came in outside of bars as well, from all sorts of places. I was working out in a gym in Melville, New York, in the early morning hours before my work day began in our Secret Service office in Long Island when we received a tip about one of the strangest PI leads I'd ever seen. A man calling himself "the Nazarene" called in to the *Howard Stern* radio show during the 6 a.m. hour and expressed a desire to kill Sen. Joseph Lieberman, saying, "That Lieberman guy has gonna [*sic*] go. He is gonna take my bullet. He's going to take it." Stern tried to warn the caller about the consequences of threatening a public figure such as Lieberman, who was the Democratic vice presidential nominee at the time and, therefore, a Secret Service protectee, but "the Nazarene" persisted, saying, "I'm telling you right now . . . You got the killer on the air . . . And that is me right here."

It wasn't long before listeners to the wildly popular radio show began lighting up the Secret Service offices with calls warning about the subject. The case quickly progressed, with the cooperation of the Stern show staff, when a trace led the New York field office agents to the home of Lawrence Christian Franco. Franco worked in a facility falling in the jurisdiction of the Long Island office where I worked, and due to the publicity surrounding the events, the investigation became an immediate priority. But instead of working with us, the New York field office agents looking at the case did a bit of big-leaguing to our tiny Long Island office. They properly notified the supervisor in charge of the Long Island office, but they steamrolled us a bit by telling us that they would handle the case, despite the connection to our district, and they basically sidelined us during the investigation. Franco was later arrested, and a pellet gun was found in the home where he resided.

The Secret Service cannot afford mistakes in PI cases, and they are always looking for an investigative edge to employ to determine whether a subject is a threat or just a big talker. Thankfully, the overwhelming majority of threat cases are just that, big talkers. I watched the evolution of threat reporting from inside the Secret Service where PI leads, early in my career, came in almost exclusively over the phone and by traditional mail, to my later years as an agent, when most of the tips came in over e-mail, and now, through social media. Regardless of the path these threats take in their route to a pair of Secret Service agent eyes, they all must be investigated. And in an effort to weed out, in the early stages of a PI investigation, the talkers from the doers, the Secret Service engaged in an ambitious project to determine what the investigative hallmarks of a credible threat were. The project, called the *Exceptional Case Study Project*, began in 1992 as an effort to generate a "research study that would produce information and ideas to assist law enforcement organizations that have protective responsibilities."[1] The project had the laudable goal of determining what specific risk factors and behavioral markers were associated with people who had "assassinated, attacked, or approached with weapons prominent persons of public status in the U.S. since 1949." By painstakingly dredging through case studies of eighty-three assassins and potential assassins and interviewing many of these subjects, the project team came to some startling conclusions about the thinking and behavior of assassins. Many of these findings changed the way the Secret Service conducted PI investigations forever. Some of the critical takeaways from the study were these:

- Many of the attackers blended into society and were not extreme social outcasts as shown in many fictional depictions of assassins.

- Although many didn't have an arrest history for violent crimes, there was a history of "harassing others" and "resentments, especially towards public officials and leaders."

- Many of the attackers had previous contact with the mental health system, ranging from psychiatric evaluation to commitment in a mental health facility.

- Many considered suicide.

- Many took an active interest in assassination as an acceptable way to act out their grievances, and some gathered "information about previous assassins."

- Many of them "took special interest in one or more public official targets."

- Few of the attackers communicated a threat to the target or to a law enforcement official before their attack, but many of them communicated their interest in an attack to someone they knew.

- Many of the attackers practiced the attack and traveled long distances in pursuit of their target while in the planning stages of the attack.

- Target shifting is common, and many of the attackers will consider more than one target, only settling on a target as an opportunity presents itself.

These were profound findings that, once the study was concluded in 1997, permanently changed how special agents interviewed, investigated, and evaluated subjects who threatened Secret Service protectees. Whether it's a Hollywood movie or a popular work of fiction where an assassin is the central antagonist, most assassins are shown as isolated social misfits, repeatedly taunting law enforcement and stalking the target they are singularly obsessed with. We've seen this character template used with the John Malkovich character in the movie *In the Line of*

Fire, and the Robert De Niro character in the movie *Taxi Driver*. Both of these characters, but specifically the Malkovich character, engage in a prolonged game of cat-and-mouse with law enforcement, which may make for good cinema, but does not reflect the realities of a PI investigation.

The findings of the study were taught to us in the Secret Service academy during agent training, and I learned to use them later in my career in a number of protective intelligence investigations I conducted. The project's findings were crucial in one particular PI investigation I was involved with while assigned to the Secret Service's Long Island office. The target came to our attention via a telephone tip from an associate of the suspect's. This associate described a number of disturbing statements the suspect had made about wishing to harm the president. When we confronted the subject in the supermarket where he worked, he immediately became hostile and lunged for a knife from the deli counter. Thankfully, my partner and I talked the subject into dropping the knife and speaking with us. We eventually made it back to the subject's apartment, and after a long conversation about everything from his musical tastes to his relationship with his family, we got him to open up to us. Keeping the subjects talking is necessary in a PI investigation because, although there may be criminal charges later, the immediate Secret Service need is not to jail the subject, but to determine if the subject is going to harm one of their protectees. Eventually, the subject disclosed that he had a fascination with a famous female musician at that time, and this set off a bunch of bells and whistles in my head. The findings of the *Exceptional Case Study*, and my subsequent protective intelligence training, had taught me that target shifting was a sign of potential danger, and this was a clear case of target promiscuity. That answer combined with his history of communicating threats to friends and associates, along with other factors, caused us great concern, and I subsequently communicated my concerns to Secret Service headquarters. I was always impressed with the seriousness of the Secret Service's commitment to their agents' judgment in PI cases. Once I made the determination that the subject was a potential threat to our protectees, I was never second-guessed. The determination was not without cost, because a finding of potential danger means more than just a lot of reporting and paperwork. It can also mean years of follow-up investigations and case monitoring, which can add up to thousands of man-hours. But back then, the Secret Service had faith in its agents and its methodology. They had trained me to look for specific signs, to combine those signs with an intense background investigation into the subject and the circumstances surrounding the threat, and to make a judgment call. I still feel, over a decade later, that I made the right call in that case, and more important, I'm convinced that the Secret Service made the right call by choosing a deeply analytical approach to threat assessment rather than being simply guided by an agent's "gut feelings." In short, protective intelligence investigations, and the corresponding threat assessment process the Secret Service teaches its agents, is something the Secret Service does better than anyone.

Given the Secret Service's extensive expertise in the evaluation of threats through the study of "targeted violence" (violent acts that are preplanned and directed at a specific person, or group of persons), the Secret Service once again waded into threat assessment to assist in helping diagnose the causes of another tragic development, the growing number of shootings and other targeted acts of violence in our nation's schools. After the horrific Columbine school shooting in 1999, the Secret Service lent its expertise to another exhaustive research study, applying some of its experiences with the *Exceptional Case Study* project, and its decades of experience in investigating and evaluating targeted threats and violence toward its protectees, to the study of school violence. The study was concluded in 2002, and some of the findings are remarkable because they point to a number of troubling similarities between the pre-attack behaviors of assassins and the pre-attack behaviors of perpetrators of targeted school violence. And whereas the perception of the presidential assassin as the societal loner, taunting law enforcement and stalking his target, was challenged by the *Exceptional Case Study*

Project, the Secret Service's study of targeted school violence rebuked the commonly held belief that these acts were acute emotional outbursts. Some of the startling findings of the report, which should concern every parent of a school-age child, included these:

- The perpetrators of school violence "often tell at least one person about their plans, give out specifics before the event takes place, and obtain weapons they need—usually from their own home or from a relative's home."[2]

- Many of the attackers did not act "impulsively" but developed a plan weeks in advance.[3]

- Many of the attackers were victims of bullying, sometimes "severe."[4]

- And shockingly, some of the attackers communicated their plans to other students who, rather than reporting the incident, actually encouraged the attacker to carry out their plans.[5]

The similarities here between assassins and perpetrators of school violence are striking. First, they aren't all socially isolated loners. The subject I determined to be a credible threat in the Long Island protective intelligence investigation had communicated his desire to harm a Secret Service protectee to associates of his, and many of the school shooters in the Secret Service study also communicated their plans to friends. In my experience interviewing the associates of potential assassins, it was commonplace for the associates of a PI subject to report to law enforcement a credible threat by the subject. But shockingly, that wasn't the case with many of the acts of targeted school violence. Some of the students who were told about the pending attacks both failed to report the plot and encouraged the attacker to carry out the act. This is a finding that should spark a conversation between every parent and his or her school-age children. There's no need to overdramatize the risk of being caught in a school shooting because, thankfully, the likelihood is extremely rare. But a commonsense conversation with our kids about learning to listen to their friends and, most important, to communicate to a responsible adult in the event that a friend talks about engaging in targeted school violence, is an essential component of keeping them and others safe.

Another similarity between assassins and targeted school violence perpetrators is the planning component. Few of these school attacks can be classified as impulsive acts; rather, similar to the assassins, many of the school attackers planned out the events in advance. That planning can involve anything from pre-attack drawings of the school, to attempts to solicit others to help carry out the violent plot. Importantly, these pre-attack behaviors can be detected if you know what you're looking for. Finally, the *Exceptional Case Study Project* found that many of the assassinations and assassination attempts were preceded by a life crisis that may have aggravated the psychological symptoms of the subjects, playing a role in the violent behavior. In a school environment, and in this new era of ubiquitous social media usage, this crisis can take the form of bullying, both online, and in person.

This is a simple conversation every parent can have with his or her child that doesn't require a government-wide public service campaign. We should all be informing our children about the damage that can be done when they decide to engage in seemingly endless online ridicule campaigns toward fellow students. This is not, and never was "harmless" childhood behavior. I'm no "safe-spacer," and I most certainly don't believe in coddling our children or helicopter parenting, but children are now living in age where they can become the objects of thousands of insults a day if someone targets them online and wishes to make a fool of them. No child has the emotional wherewithal to handle that kind of harassment, and shouldn't have to. The Secret Service study showed us all the damage that this type of behavior can cause, and it's something every responsible parent should take to heart.

PART 3

HOW TO FIX THE SECRET SERVICE

15

WORTHY OF TRUST AND CONFIDENCE

THE SECRET SERVICE NEEDS TO LEARN HOW TO WIN again and embrace their motto "Worthy of trust and confidence." For the sake of the country, the Secret Service needs to return to better times, when special agent resignations were so rare that when word spread about an agent's resignation, fellow agents would ask, "Why would he do that?" Despite the small size of the Secret Service relative to the other federal law enforcement agencies, they serve two critical missions for the maintenance of our constitutional republic: they secure the life of the president of the United States, and they secure the integrity of the nation's money supply. Unfortunately, the expanding mission of the

Secret Service, and the growing threat environment, requires that the Secret Service forfeit portions of their current investigative mission in order to fulfill their protection mission. The Secret Service does not have the manpower, or the time, to be involved in credit-card fraud investigations, counterfeit currency investigations, electronic crimes investigations, 419 fraud (e-mail and paper mail scams where innocent victims are solicited by phony Nigerian "princes" looking to give them millions of dollars in exchange for their bank account numbers), major events security, and protective intelligence investigations. The Secret Service does presidential protection better than any government agency in the world, and that's where they add substantial value for U.S. tax-payers, not in doing financial crimes investigations, which can easily be absorbed the FBI.

Although the transition would be painful at first for many of the current crop of special agents, many of whom have grown to enjoy criminal investigative work and have never known a time when they weren't expected to conduct criminal investigations, it would benefit both the agents and Secret Service management to focus on high-value-added activities. This includes presidential protection, major event security, critical infrastructure protection, electronic crimes, and protective intelligence operations. Giving up their counterfeit, credit-card fraud, and 419-fraud investigative work would allow the Secret Service to refocus its mission and leverage the skills it has acquired from decades of presidential protection work across complementary activities (such as critical infrastructure protection and major events security).

When a Secret Service agent does security advance work for one of their protectees, one of the tasks they regularly perform is a thorough security evaluation of the location the protectee is going to visit. Agents look at the building's air-intake system, the fire-suppression system, the location of crash bar doors (crash bar doors close automatically and prevent stairways from filling with smoke in a fire) to ensure that escape routes are accessible in the event of a fire, the network connectivity of the building to make sure that critical information technology systems cannot be hacked, the location of the firebox, the location of the security cameras, and more. After decades of conducting security advances such as this, in buildings and facilities all across the country, the Secret Service would be the ideal agency to lead a national collaborative effort between private industry and government to secure our nation's critical infrastructure. This effort wouldn't require any additional taxpayer money, and it would be completely voluntary for private industry. But it would help the Secret Service in a few ways. If the Secret Service were to give up its financial crimes and counterfeit investigations, it would free up large blocks of time for Secret Service agents. Some presidents travel frequently, such as President Clinton, and some travel only when necessary, such as President Reagan. The Secret Service has to be prepared for the worst-case travel scenario, however, and doesn't have the luxury of dismissing its workforce and then rehiring them when the campaign and presidential travel seasons heat up. The Secret Service is no different from a big-city fire department in this regard. Fire departments do not start fires to prove their worth. They wait for a fire event, and they are vigilantly prepared to respond to that event. The same principle should apply to the Secret Service with a presidential visit. Allowing the Secret Service, in the downtime between protection operations, to work with private industry to help provide security consultation for the nation's power plants, critical electrical infrastructure, critical Internet hubs, and other infrastructure assets necessary for our national safety and survival, would allow agents the opportunity to fine-tune their site security skills while developing networks of industry contacts within their respective field office districts. This would benefit the agency as a whole when a Secret Service protectee visits their districts.

This would also fill a major hole in our nation's security. As our society has evolved from a dependency on agriculture and manufacturing to a more diversified economy dependent on service sectors and connectivity, the line between private and public has blurred with regard to critical infrastructure national security. For example, no one doubts the need to secure our nation's military facilities and government buildings, such as the White House and our courts. But with our growing dependency on energy and Internet connectivity networks, isn't it critical that we also focus on securing our nation's electrical grid and Internet connectivity, despite the fact that they are not government assets in the traditional sense? Now, to be clear, I am a strong advocate for limited government, and I am not suggesting anything more than making the Secret Service available to consult with the private industry representatives responsible for our energy grid, critical Internet infrastructure, national ports, and our other vital national security interests to assist in providing security guidance and best practices. The Secret Service is perfectly suited for this role because they are already involved in similar ventures through their leadership role in the coordination of the nation's electronic crimes task forces in the investigation and prosecution of Internet crimes, and their role with the Department of Homeland Security as a partner in the US-CERT (United States Computer Emergency Readiness Team). The US-CERT is a collaborative venture between federal law enforcement and the technology industry to "analyze threats, and exchange critical cybersecurity information with trusted partners around the world."[6]

The US-CERT is a model for handling the increasingly blurry line between critical government assets and critical private industry assets in this new era of essential worldwide connectivity. The Secret Service uses this network of willing private and government partners to spread information about the latest cyber-vulnerabilities and trends in Internet-based crimes, all at little expense to the taxpayer. Expanding this model into business spheres outside of the technology industry, such as the energy sector, is a logical next step. The Secret Service wouldn't be required to do anything more than to provide unclassified security consultation to willing private industry partners, and private industry would then be responsible for investing in the necessary security upgrades using their own capital.

Undoubtedly, this effort to move the Secret Service away from financial crimes and into collaborative critical-infrastructure security wouldn't come without friction. A knowledgeable defense expert associate of mine who served in the Reagan administration, once described the problem for me. He explained that our nation has a glaring hole in our electrical-transmission infrastructure because of the threat of an electromagnetic pulse (EMP) attack generated from an atmospheric nuclear weapon detonation. This scenario may seem far-fetched, but it is very real in the eyes of our geopolitical adversaries, who understand that an attack such as this would wipe out electrical power for millions of Americans instantaneously. In addition, our national capacity to rebuild the electrical transformers that would be damaged in an EMP attack would be severely compromised, and as a result, it could take years to get the nation's electrical power back. Literally millions of Americans could die if an attack like this were successfully implemented. With a catastrophic threat such as this, a reasonable person would conclude that our nation had already developed a thorough plan, in conjunction with the energy sector, to harden up our electrical grid to ensure that it could still function after being exposed to an EMP attack. But despite some efforts to solve the problem (notably, a recent push by the U.S. government's Defense Advanced Research Project, DARPA, in conjunction with BAE Systems to develop "alternative communication networks that would come into use in case of a cyberattack on the US electrical grid"[7]), the nation's electrical grid is still largely unprotected from this catastrophic threat. One of the reasons behind this intransigence is an ongoing dispute about who should absorb the costs for this effort: private industry, the government, or both. The same disputes would likely emerge from a new Secret Service–led effort to provide best practices and guidance for private industry. Once a government agency such as the Secret Service provides security advice and guidance, private industry may hesitate when they see the costs of security upgrades. Even worse, many might avoid consultation with the Secret Service at all, figuring that ignorance is bliss. If they are told about holes in their security plans, and they fail to act, many industry figures may be rightly concerned about lawsuits in the event of a security incident. These are real concerns but they can be remedied with strict operating and disclosure rules for private organizations joining the consortium.

Reforming the mission of the Secret Service should also include an expansion of their protective intelligence role. Although forfeiting the financial crimes and counterfeiting missions is essential to freeing up limited Secret Service manpower assets, they must hold on to the investigative responsibilities for threats to their protectees. Protective intelligence investigations are complicated investigations that require a Secret Service agent to dig deep into the mind of a potential assassin to determine the subject's intent. There is no room for mistakes in these PI investigations, and learning to competently conduct them can provide an agent with essential insight into the psychological states of the people wishing to do their protectees harm. After interviewing multiple suspects accused of threatening the president and other Secret Service protectees, I became all-too-familiar with "the look," that blank stare a sociopath, with no attachment to any moral code, gives you when you are interviewing him about a threat he made to the president. You learn quickly when dealing with sociopaths, a category into which many potential assassins fall, not to try to get a sincere apology or a morally relevant explanation of why they did what they did. Most of them did it because they wanted to, because it filled some physical or mental unmet need, regardless of the pain they were looking to cause. They are not overwhelmed by a sense of shame and sorrow for their actions because the moral code most of us live by does not equally govern their actions. These are critical skills that translate directly to the effectiveness of the protection mission.

I recall multiple instances of agents on posts within a secure perimeter, telling supervisors that something "just wasn't right" about a person, and later being proven right when the person was interviewed. Although not all of these people were assassins or terrorists, many of them were there exclusively to cause trouble for the Secret Service. There's no good substitute for experience in protective intelligence investigations. It's possible that what set off many of these agents' "trouble antenna" was their ability to observe barely quantifiable behavioral indicators that they had experience in dealing with from their investigations of threat cases.

Keeping protective intelligence investigations under the Secret Service umbrella, while turning over financial crimes and counterfeit investigations to other federal agencies, will also ensure that the Secret Service allocates more of its limited manpower to the exploding number of social media threats driven by President Trump's unprecedented use of social media platforms. President Trump personally communicates regularly using Twitter, unlike past presidents, who used the platform through official channels, and this has invited a growing number of threatening responses. Twitter threats are nothing new to the Secret Service, but the public knows the president personally uses Twitter, and many PI subjects have decided to take the opportunity to personally threaten him by responding. Regardless of what the Secret Service says publicly, this has put an incredible strain on the agency because they cannot afford to ignore threats simply because they originate from a Twitter user. I fear that this threat stream emanating from social media will only grow in the future as President Trump redefines the role of social media within the presidency. And the future growth in social media threats will require a manpower response from the Secret Service. With government-wide budget cuts likely coming in the future due to our nearly $20 trillion national debt, big increases in Secret Service hiring are unlikely. Therefore, it's critical that the Secret Service upper management get ahead of this problem today by looking at reallocating financial crimes manpower assets to protective intelligence.

Another lingering problem for the Secret Service that requires an immediate fix is their overreliance on internal promotions for their upper management team. The use of strictly internal promotions to fill the headquarters management staff of the Secret Service has promoted a "groupthink" atmosphere with no set of outside eyes to critically analyze major decisions. I place the blame for the destruction of Secret Service morale largely on a series of disastrous decisions made by the headquarters management teams over the past two decades. First, the decision to expand the Secret Service portfolio of responsibilities by taking on security responsibilities for significant national security events designated NSSEs was an avoidable mistake. Although the skill set Secret Service agents have due to their protection responsibilities is a strong fit for a coordination role in securing NSSE events, this role should be strictly advisory, similar to what I proposed for the private industry/Secret Service critical infrastructure security consortium. Having well-trained, and taxpayer-funded, Secret Service agents work as security guards at events such as the Salt Lake City Olympics was a mistake that did substantial damage to special agent morale as the NSSE assignments piled up. Secret Service management erred terribly in not taking a stand on this earlier, when the complaints from the agents on the ground began to pile up. They should have resolutely refused to provide special agent manpower, essential to keeping the president, and their growing number of protectees safe, for security at events that had no nexus whatsoever to the Secret Service's core protection mission.

Second, the decision by Secret Service management, many of whom had relocated many times themselves, to continue the destructive policy of requiring relocations for continued promotion within the agency, was one that still boggles the mind. Nearly every agent I spoke with during my time in the New York field office, the Secret Service training center, the PPD, and while on the road conducting protection operations, absolutely despised this policy. Yet, headquarters managers refused to change the relocation policy and only made token changes to the "career track" options, which had little impact on the real lives of agents who loved the Secret Service but also loved their families and refused to repeatedly relocate them. Hundreds of talented special agents were lost to other federal agencies due to this misguided policy, and no one was held accountable for this disaster.

By filling some Senior Executive Service management positions within the Secret Service with people who have never served in the agency, it would finally be possible to get a critical set of outside eyes on the operations of the agency—eyes that have not been subjected to the infamous "because that's the way we've always done it" groupthink trap that currently pervades the agency. Military and business leaders have not "always done it" the Secret Service way, and although there are no guarantees, outsiders to the Secret Service would be more likely to ask critical questions, such as "Why the hell are we moving agents around the country, spending a fortune to do so, and getting nothing more than mass resignations and crushed morale to show for it?" I assure you, a successful business or military leader would not accept an answer such as "Because that's the way we've always done it." The excuse for not doing this has traditionally been, "The Secret Service has a unique and hard-to-understand protection mission, and an outside manager from the agency wouldn't understand it." Yes, the protection mission is incredibly complicated, but so is building a modern motor vehicle, and yet, no one expects the CEO of a major car company to be able to walk on the assembly line and build the vehicle himself. The upper management of any organization doesn't have to grasp every nuance of the organization they run, but it's essential that they lead the organization by providing strategic vision and audacious, visionary goals.

Leadership means a lot of different things to a lot of different people. But you can be assured that your organization's leadership has failed when the overwhelming majority of your workforce cites the lack of leadership as a problem in employee surveys, and the documented history of critical decision making leaves behind a trail of mission failure, employee attrition, and bruised morale. New leadership, from outside of the Secret Service, isn't limited by the tunnel vision "groupthink" that is all too common throughout today's Secret Service. Many of the executive management staff of today's Secret Service grew up together in the agency and learned from one another. Many were successful security advance agents who taught others how to navigate the difficult world of presidential protection. But presidential protection agents, who excel at the mechanics of security advance work, may not be best suited as upper-level managers tasked with dealing with Congress on the mission of the Secret Service, with dealing with the Secret Service workforce on quality-of-life issues, or with dealing with the media when there is a Secret Service crisis. Sometimes, having nothing but insiders managing an organization encourages repetition of the same mistakes because no one realizes that a mistake has even been made. It reminds me of a story I once heard about a junior firefighter who survived a massive outdoor forest fire while his senior firefighter associates perished. One of the reasons given was that the senior firefighters were trained to never leave behind their gear, and therefore they tragically perished when the flames engulfed them as they were weighed down by the bulky gear. The junior firefighter didn't respond the same way. He ditched his gear and escaped.

Sometimes, inexperience with mistakes can be an advantage, and in the case of the Secret Service, it's time to try something new as the mistakes pile up. America cannot afford to lose another president, and fixing the Secret Service is the *only* way to ensure that we don't.

NOTES

INTRODUCTION

1. Kevin Liptak, Michelle Kosinski, and Chris Frates, "Drunk Secret Service Agents Crash into White House Barrier," CNN, March 12, 2015, http://www.cnn.com/2015/03/11/politics/drunk-secret-service-agents-white-house.

2. Mhairi MacFarlane, "Watch Video of 'drunk' Secret Service Agents Nudging White House Bomb Scene Barrier with Vehicle," *Mirror*, March 24, 2015, http://www.mirror.co.uk/news/world-news/watch-video-drunk-secret-service-5394235.

CHAPTER 1: THE SPECIAL AGENT MESS

1. Mike Jones, "Aaron Rodgers: "You Have to Learn How to Win in the Playoffs," *Washington Post*, January 7, 2016, https://www.washingtonpost.com/news/football-insider/wp/2016/01/07/aaron-rodgers-you-have-to-learn-how-to-win-in-the-playoffs/?utm_term=.1b9f63b37b75.

2. The White House Office of the Press Secretary, "Fact Sheet: Combating Terrorism: Presidential Decision Directive 62," May 22, 1998, https://fas.org/irp/offdocs/pdd-62.htm.

3. 106th Congress, "Presidential Threat Protection Act of 2000," US Government Printing Office, https://www.gpo.gov/fdsys/pkg/PLAW-106publ544/html/PLAW-106publ544.htm.

4. Joe Davidson, "Why Is Secret Service Morale So Low?" *Washington Post*, December 8, 2015, https://www.washingtonpost.com/news/federal-eye/wp/2015/12/08/why-is-secret-service-morale-so-low/?utm_term=.25da9d786abd.

5. Joseph Hagin et al., "Executive Summary to Report from the United States Secret Service Protective Mission Panel to the Secretary of Homeland Security," December 15, 2014, https://www.dhs.gov/sites/default/files/publications/14_1218_usss_pmp.pdf, 3.

CHAPTER 2: THE UNIFORMED DIVISION OFFICER MESS

1. Hagin et al., "Executive Summary to Report from the United States Secret Service Protective Mission Panel to the Secretary of Homeland Security," 5.

CHAPTER 3: THE EVOLVING THREATS FROM THE "BIG SIX"

1. "Report: Hillary Leaves 9/11 Mem'l Early Due to 'Medical Episode," Fox News *Insider*, September 11, 2016, http://insider.foxnews.com/2016/09/11/hillary-clinton-reportedly-leaves-911-memorial-ceremony-early-due-medical-episode.

CHAPTER 4: THE THREAT OF A TACTICAL ASSAULT ON THE PRESIDENT

1. Ironically, it's the difficult-to-articulate "street sense" developed over time that I believe causes a lot of problems with the recording of stop-and-frisk interactions. Many cops know why they stopped a person, but when forced to recall the details even moments later, they forget some of the specifics due to the stress of the situation, and they subsequently cannot repeat what the reasonable suspicion was that led to the stop.

2. Benjamin Weingarten, "America's 'Known Wolf' Jihadist Problem: Why Haven't We Learned from Our Mistakes?" *Counter Jihad Report*, April 20, 2017, https://counterjihadreport.com/2017/04/20/americas-known-wolf-jihadist-problem-why-havent-we-learned-from-our-mistakes/.

CHAPTER 8: TRUMP AND TWITTER: A BLESSING AND A CURSE

1. Donald J. Trump, tweet to Dan Bongino, Twitter, August 10, 2016, https://twitter.com/realdonaldtrump/status/763391459110313984?lang=en.

2. Fox News Watters' World, April 23, 2017. http://nation.foxnews.com/2017/04/23/trumps-social-media-director-battling-fake-news-we-re-driving-liberals-insane.

CHAPTER 10: THE BROKEN WHITE HOUSE SECURITY PLAN

1. Marisa Schultz, "Secret Service Wants to Build $8M Fake White House for Training," *New York Post*, March 17, 2015, http://nypost.com/2015/03/17/secret-service-wants-to-build-8m-fake-white-house-for-training/.

CHAPTER 14: YOUR CHILD'S SCHOOL IS SAFER BECAUSE THE SECRET SERVICE STUDIED ASSASSINS

1. Robert A. Fein and Bryan Vossekuil, *Preventing Assassination: A Monograph: Secret Service Exceptional Case Study Project*, May 1997, https://www.ncjrs.gov/pdffiles1/Photocopy/167224NCJRS.pdf.

2. "Preventing School Shootings: A Summary of a U.S. Secret Service Safe School Initiative Report," *NIJ Journal* 248 (2002): 11, https://www.ncjrs.gov/pdffiles1/jr000248c.pdf.

3. Ibid., 12.

4. Ibid., 14.

5. Ibid.

6. "About Us," the US-CERT website, accessed May 19, 2017, https://www.us-cert.gov/about-us.

7. Kris Osborn, "DARPA Tasks BAE with Workaround to Secure the Power Grid in the Event of Massive Attack," Defense Systems, April 13, 2017, https://defensesystems.com/articles/2017/04/13/grid.aspx.

INDEX